EARL SCRUGGS

AND FOGGY MOUNTAIN BREAKDOWN

THE MAKING OF AN
AMERICAN CLASSIC

THOMAS GOLDSMITH

**UNIVERSITY OF
ILLINOIS PRESS**
Urbana, Chicago, and Springfield

Publication of this book was supported in part by a grant from the
Judith McCulloh Endowment for American Music.

Library of Congress Cataloging-in-Publication Data
Names: Goldsmith, Thomas, 1952– author.
Title: Earl Scruggs and Foggy mountain breakdown: the making of an
American classic / Thomas Goldsmith.
Description: Urbana: University of Illinois Press, 2019. | Series: Music
in American life | Includes bibliographical references and index. |
Summary: "Less than three minutes long and involving no lyrics,
"Foggy Mountain Breakdown" is a banjo-led song that changed the
face of American music. Composed and recorded by Earl Scruggs in
1949, the song went on to transform and modernize folk culture of
the early 20th century, its effects extending far beyond bluegrass.
The captivating sound of the piece helped rejuvenate the banjo,
an instrument that had been vanishing from the mainstream of
American music; its unforgettable twang and cadence ushered the
banjo and backwoods into American popular culture by providing
the soundtrack for *The Beverly Hillbillies* and *Bonnie and Clyde*; its
close relationship to "Blue Grass Breakdown," a song composed by
Scruggs' one-time bandleader Bill Monroe, illustrates the fungible
nature of intellectual property in the early days of country music;
and the song's advanced compositional techniques and technical
difficulty helped distinguish Scruggs as one of a small handful of
principals of acoustic music. Relying on primary sources, including
interviews with Scruggs and his wife and manager, Louise, as well
as with Curly Seckler, the only surviving musician from the 1949
recording, this project examines the story surrounding "Foggy
Mountain Breakdown." Along the way, Goldsmith reveals much
about Scruggs's career and the evolution of his influential style. No
such examination about Scruggs or his famous song exists, so this
project is positioned to make a strong contribution to the history of
bluegrass"— Provided by publisher.
Identifiers: LCCN 2019025460 (print) | LCCN 2019025461 (ebook) | ISBN
9780252042966 (cloth) | ISBN 9780252084782 (paperback) | ISBN
9780252051821 (ebook other)
Subjects: LCSH: Scruggs, Earl. | Scruggs, Earl. Foggy mountain
breakdown. | Banjoists—United States—Biography. | Bluegrass
musicians—United States—Biography.
Classification: LCC ML419.S38 G65 2019 (print) | LCC ML419.S38 (ebook)
| DDC 787.8/81642092 [B]—dc23
LC record available at https://lccn.loc.gov/2019025460
LC ebook record available at https://lccn.loc.gov/2019025461

Mark how one string, sweet husband to another,
Strikes each in each by mutual ordering;
Resembling sire and child and happy mother,
Who, all in one, one pleasing note do sing . . .

— "Sonnet 8," William Shakespeare

CONTENTS

 **ACKNOWLEDGMENTS**

This book exists because of the generosity and friendship that Earl and Louise Scruggs and family showed me for many years in Nashville, a relationship that continued in the years after I returned to my native state of North Carolina. I first approached Earl and Louise as they sat alone at a table during an event at Johnny Cash's house (to promote June Carter's book about her mother Maybelle's cooking). We bonded as fellow North Carolinians and music fans. The face-to-face interviews I had with Earl form the heart of this book.

Beyond that starting place, major thanks go to Jim Mills, to Béla Fleck, to Greg Earnest, and to the indefatigable source of energy known as F. H. Flash of Flint Hill, North Carolina. They are among the leaders in the study of Earl, his banjo, and his art.

Thanks to my editor, Laurie Matheson of the University of Illinois Press, who ended our first, hasty conversation about this book by saying, "I guess if anybody can do it, you can." Valuable help also came from press staff, including Julianne Rose Laut, Nancy Albright, Roger Cunningham, Justin Hubbart, Angela Burton, Jennifer Argo, and Heather Gernenz.

Scholar and picker Murphy Henry and my best friend, Marshall Wyatt, provided invaluable feedback and encouragement to early drafts. If mistakes remain, they are on me. The anonymous reader for UIP who raised serious questions about my first draft should get credit for many later improvements. I enjoyed and benefited from trading Flatt and Scruggs lore with Penny Parsons as she worked on her Curly Seckler biography. Thanks to my friend Stacy Chandler for a round of copy editing that used both her daily journalism and music expertise.

Banjothon leaders Mike Johnson, Larry Mathis, and Barry Palmer showed me friendship and hospitality, starting in the days when the event was still held at a senior center in Maryville, Tennessee.

Thanks to Anne Tyler, who in a few lines gave me a sense of what it means to finish a book.

Special thanks to Charley Pennell for his stellar work in indexing this book.

Research resources included Ken Beck, Bob Carlin, Walter and Christie Carter, Carter Vintage Instruments, Nashville, Tennessee; Greg Earnest, Pre-war Gibson Mastertone Banjos website, Atlanta; East Tennessee Historical Society, Knoxville, Tennessee; Ranger Doug Green, George Gruhn, Gruhn Guitars, Nashville, Tennessee; Shelby resident and historian Jim Kunkle; Brent Lamons, picker and historian; Teresa Leonard, *News & Observer*; Lexington Public Library, Lexington, Kentucky; Paley Center for Media, New York City, New York; Brian Powers, Cincinnati Public Library; bluegrass journalism dean Neil V. Rosenberg; John Rumble, Country Music Foundation; Elliott Ruther, Cincinnati USA Music Heritage Foundation; The Scruggs Center, Shelby, North Carolina; Joti Rockwell, associate professor of music, Pomona College; Wake County Public Library, Raleigh, North Carolina; Ben Runkle of Raleigh, North Carolina; J. T. Scruggs of Shelby, North Carolina; Steve Weiss, Aaron Smithers, and crew, Southern Folklife Collection, UNC–Chapel Hill; and Marshall Wyatt, Old Hat Records.

Interviews, some conducted in years past for other projects, included Eddie Adcock; Walter and Christie Carter; J. D. Crowe; Jerry Douglas; Béla Fleck; Alice Gerrard; George Gruhn; John Hedgecoth; Jerry Keys; Gene Knight; Brent Lamons; Dan Loftin; Jesse McReynolds; Steve Martin; Jim Mills; Tim O'Brien; Sonny Osborne; Earl, Louise, and Gary Scruggs; J. T. Scruggs; Curly Seckler; Sammy Shelor; Lily Werbin; and especially Mac Wiseman, who remembered so much. Sadly for people who love this music, Seckler and Wiseman died as this book neared publication, and are much missed. Special thanks go to the late Bill Monroe, who talked generously to me on many occasions after I came up with some good questions.

Finally, thanks times one million go to my beloved wife, Renee, and to my excellent children, Kelsey, Hudson, and Nate, for sticking with me and for believing that there must be a purpose to the several years I spent on this book.

EARL
SCRUGGS
AND FOGGY MOUNTAIN BREAKDOWN

1

OUT TO FOLLOW
SCRUGGS'S PATH

In Cleveland County, North Carolina, a few years ago, a worn white farmhouse stood neglected and unmarked on a two-lane road outside the small town of Boiling Springs. In November twilight, the house in the old Flint Hill community evoked a fine glow of memory and history, though its paint was peeling and its masonry crumbled. A visitor could walk down into fields that a boy named Earl Scruggs plowed for the family cotton crop in the 1930s. Cars and trucks drove by, and people waved, perhaps accustomed to visitors at the modest home.

The scene brought back the years in the 1920s and '30s when Scruggs, born in 1924, lived on the farm with his parents, George and Lula, and his two brothers and two sisters. It was here that Earl had a substantial musical breakthrough on the five-string banjo when still a child. And just a few minutes' walk away, on the wooded banks of the Broad River, Scruggs gave some of his earliest performances. He played for diners at a "fish camp," an open-air, lamp-lit eating place that he could still conjure up decades later.

It was here, in Flint Hill, in Boiling Springs, and along the Broad River, that the story of "Foggy Mountain Breakdown" began. The banjo tune was to play a major role in making Scruggs famous and in preserving the country string music and the banjo he picked so well.

The second floor of 811 Race Street in downtown Cincinnati, Ohio, contains the former home of the Herzog Recording Studio, where forward-thinking record man Murray Nash made the first recording of "Foggy Mountain Breakdown" on December 11, 1949. Scruggs on banjo was backed by his guitarist partner Lester Flatt and the rest of their Foggy Mountain Boys band.

The walls of the Herzog studio, where Flatt and Scruggs, Patti Page, Hank Williams and others cut records, remain intact, although the control room and recording space are no longer separated. Only a piano said to have been played by Williams keeps its place from the studio's heyday.

Second-floor windows overlook downtown Cincinnati. A visitor can get a sense of what it was like for the Foggy Mountain Boys to pull up on Race Street, on a day off from their busy touring schedule out of Lexington, Kentucky. Although the original equipment is gone, the place still offers a bluegrass fan the chance to "stand on the rock where Moses stood," in the words of an old gospel song.

These places, and many others, were part of my journey to track the story of "Foggy Mountain Breakdown" and to understand the impact it has made. Of course, that meant tracing the story of Earl Scruggs as well.

Recorded in that basic studio in Cincinnati, the tune has won singular status through the years. In just a few examples, honors came in 2000 from National Public Radio, which named "Foggy Mountain Breakdown" one of the 100 most important American musical works of the 20th century. On April 5, 2005, Librarian of Congress James H. Billington named "Foggy Mountain Breakdown" to the National Recording Registry, denoting recordings that are "culturally, historically or aesthetically significant." And it's the only tune to win two Grammys in performances by the same artist.

The trail of "Foggy Mountain Breakdown" has led me down a thousand paths I wouldn't otherwise have encountered. It meant doing what I love—chasing facts and shreds of facts until I believe I've put them into a meaningful whole. I've spent much of my career in hard news but have gotten the chance to write about bluegrass music off and on since 1985, when I was moved to the full-time staff as a reporter for *The Ten-*

nessean, Nashville's morning daily. Most of the field's important artists lived around Nashville and were willing to talk to a journalist about their music. Among those were singers and pickers whose stories dated to the years when this style of music came together, just after World War II. I got the chance to talk to figures such as Scruggs, Bill Monroe, Mac Wiseman, Jim & Jesse McReynolds, Ralph Stanley, and Bobby and Sonny Osborne, as well as up-and-comers such as Sam Bush, Jerry Douglas, Béla Fleck, Ricky Skaggs, Claire Lynch, Alison Krauss and Union Station, and the Nashville Bluegrass Band.

Years later, Neil V. Rosenberg approved my picking up work on a book that he had conceived, a collection of good writing in the field. The University of Illinois published *The Bluegrass Reader* in 2004 to good response, including the International Bluegrass Music Association's award for print journalist of the year.

This book began with the idea of bringing together several resonant stories about the best-known songs of bluegrass, numbers like "Blue Moon of Kentucky," "Rocky Top," and "Foggy Mountain Breakdown." When I decided to concentrate instead on Scruggs's banjo tune, the process involved gathering previous interviews and lore, and then hitting the road and phone for more research and further interviews. Another chunk of fact gathering took place on line, where newly digitized newspapers and magazines from the 1930s and beyond offered details and insights into Scruggs's origins and life path.

===

Earl Eugene Scruggs, born January 6, 1924, came from a deeply country background to touch American music and culture during many decades. His picking started "winning little awards" when he was six years old and garnered wild, shouted responses by the time of his first appearances at the Grand Ole Opry in 1945. Scruggs's long career brought his music to live audiences, regional and national radio, top-selling records, syndicated and network television, and the soundtrack of the genre-disrupting movie *Bonnie and Clyde*.

Even the banjo he played, a prewar Gibson Mastertone, became the center of a cult of players and collectors who still come together in meetings, seminars, and stores to learn ever more about Scruggs and these banjos.

A soft-spoken man and an acute thinker, Scruggs made a singular contribution to perfecting and keeping alive the rural, almost primal music of the Carolina piedmont. The story of "Foggy Mountain Breakdown" stretches from the Carolinas of the 1930s to the present day. Its saga took place in locations from Boiling Springs to Manhattan, from a Parisian restaurant to small Texas towns of the 1960s. The voices and places along the way showed me the variegated influences that came together in the lasting success of "Foggy Mountain Breakdown."

"I GREW UP
AROUND A BANJO"

Boiling Springs, North Carolina, had but one stoplight in the 1920s and
'30s, when Betty Jenkins Washburn was growing up not far from Earl
Scruggs's home. In an interview in 2015, Washburn, 89, remembered Earl
as an elementary school classmate. People already knew he was a banjo
picker.[1]

"He was really shy, real nice, clean-cut, a farm boy," she said. "They lived
down in the country toward the river on a farm."

Flint Hill was just a mile or so from "downtown" Boiling Springs, but
people there knew who was from "down in the country" and who was from
the town. Eighty years later, Washburn, the daughter of a traveling evange-
list, laughed at the idea that little Boiling Springs counted as "town." When
she was grown, Washburn and her husband became close to Earl's brother
Horace and his wife, Maida. As time passed, people in Boiling Springs heard
firsthand about Earl's steady rise to stardom.

"He had talent, didn't he?" Betty Washburn said. "We didn't know it
then. Just knew that he and Horace and some of the boys got together and
played music."

Pictures of young Earl show a round-faced, thoughtful boy. He was the
youngest in a brood of three boys and two girls, later joined by stepsister

Venie Mae. All were expected to work around the farm. Scruggs's stories of those days entwined music with accounts of plowing, milking, and getting breakfast for the mules. Often the work came between Earl and music, especially when he had to complete his schoolwork, too.

The nearest place of any size was Shelby, the county seat and a courthouse town where families like the Scruggses might go to shop and visit with friends on Saturdays. Although politics and business bustled in Shelby, Cleveland County people mostly worked in raising and processing cotton. During the decade when Scruggs was born, Cleveland County went from producing 8,000 bales a year to 80,000 bales.[2]

"I was grown before I ever knew that North Carolina was the tobacco state," Scruggs said. "Where I was raised, it was cotton. We didn't grow tobacco up there. That showed you how rural it was."[3]

Scruggs's roots ran deep in this country. His father, George Elam Scruggs, child of David and Sarah Green Scruggs, was born in Cleveland County on January 10, 1876. George Scruggs was a landowner, bookkeeper, churchman, and farmer. In 1920, according to Census records, the household also included a hired man, Clifton B. Hamrick.

On November 4, 1906, at 30, George Scruggs married the former Georgia Lula Ruppe, known as Lula, a bride at 13.[4] Late to marry, George Scruggs died early, at 52, on October 10, 1928.[5] As the youngest child of his family, Earl knew his father for the fewest years.

"My dad played a little bit with the banjo and fiddle, but he died when I was four, so I don't remember any of his playing," Scruggs said. "He died of lung cancer, but he was in bed eight months before he died, so I wasn't much past three years old when he was up on his feet."[6]

An October 18, 1928, obituary in the *Forest City Courier* called George Elam Scruggs "a Prominent Man of Boiling Springs Community and Church Clerk.

"Mr. Scruggs was clerk of the Boiling Springs Baptist Church for a number of years, and his quiet unassuming manner won the respect and admiration of all with whom he came in contact," the paper said. He had been "one of the best known and popular citizens of Boiling Springs."

≡

Brother Horace, nearly two years older, supplied Earl with pieces of the memories he had lost so painfully.

"He said Dad used to come in the room—Mama wanted everybody up for breakfast, you know, while it was hot. He'd come in taking a banjo to wake me and Horace up in the morning."

Along with this wonderful image, Earl inherited his father's legacy of achievement and musicality. Blessed with musical parents, the Scruggs siblings all played music. George Scruggs had played fiddle, and banjo in the down-picking style, of African origin, that was common all over the South. Lula Ruppe Scruggs played pump organ and piano. Older brothers Horace and Junius, or Junie, as well as sisters Eula Mae and Ruby all played banjo and guitar. The ideas, techniques, and sounds of music were all around him.

"I grew up around a banjo," Earl Scruggs said.

Gary Scruggs, the oldest of Earl's three sons, often heard about the times when the Scruggses of Flint Hill gathered for music. "The family members in Dad's youth all played music to some degree," he said. "Dad and his brother Horace especially played a lot together. Horace played rhythm acoustic guitar, and he played it very well. The older siblings, brother Junie and sisters Eula Mae and Ruby, all married at young ages and moved out, so there was not as much playing music with them as there was with Horace."[7]

The family's life took an irreparable turn when George Scruggs died of cancer.

"My mother raised us, me being the youngest," Earl Scruggs said. "We mainly raised what we ate and then grew the cotton for a cash crop. That was just our country lifestyle. Getting by was really what we were doing."

Earl began playing the banjo about the time his father died. "I loved music long as I can remember," he said. "I played before I even knew what radio was."[8]

Because Earl was so small, he couldn't hold the banjo in his lap, the way older players did. He developed a method that involved sitting with legs crossed, resting the banjo's body on the floor and stretching his left hand up to reach the instrument's frets. "The only way I could pick Junie's banjo, or the old one my father played, was to sit on the floor with the body part of the banjo to my right and slide it around quite a bit, depending on what position on the neck I was attempting to play."

In addition to that sitarlike approach, Scruggs tried another method to play an instrument that was really too large for him. He explained it to student journalist Norman Draper of the University of North Carolina's *Daily Tar Heel* in 1972.

"Most of the time I would use a chair, you know, sit in a chair and put the box part of the banjo in another chair and pick it like that," Scruggs said. "My oldest brother had kind of a fancy banjo. It was cheap, but it was expensive for him at that time. When he was gone, I'd get on the bed or pull up a couple of chairs and put it in one chair and I'd sit in the other chair and pick the banjo."

In a home that in its early years had no radio or record player, music provided diversion and relief from the work of farm life. "Well, we had a banjo in the house, along with guitar and autoharp," Scruggs said. "My father's old open-back. It's in the Country Music Hall of Fame and Museum now; about a three-dollar banjo. And you know, sitting by the fire in the winter time by yourself, it made pretty good noise."

George Scruggs's banjo has been moved from the Country Hall of Fame and Museum to the Scruggs Center in Shelby. The instrument Earl used for most of his career, the 1930 Gibson Granada Mastertone called "The Banjo" by the faithful, attracts visitors at the Country Music Hall of Fame and Museum in Nashville.

———

By age six, according to his brother Horace, Earl took part in his first picking contest, held in Hamrick Auditorium on the grounds of what's now Gardner-Webb University in Boiling Springs.

"Hamrick was the only place around here that was large enough for any kind of gathering," Horace said.[9] Young Earl walked the two miles from Flint Hill to Boiling Springs for the contest, banjo on his back. He won, but later came to think it was his youth that won him recognition.

"I got some kind of little prize that night, playing 'Cripple Creek' or something," he said.[10]

The music that Earl heard continued to play in his mind, over and again, sometimes taking on new forms as it repeated.

"The banjo stayed on my mind just about all the time," he said. "One reason, I guess, that it stayed on my mind so much is that on the farm, we didn't have the privileges that young boys have now. They can sit around and practice five or six hours a day. Back then, we couldn't hardly get our schoolwork in for the farming.

"So about the only times I got to pick was a little bit before breakfast and sometimes, if I felt like it, a little bit during the noon hour while I was resting. And a little bit on weekends or on rainy days, when I could sit and pick all I cared to.

"But I would plow from one end of the field to the other with tunes running through my head. When I'd get back to the house, as soon as I could get hold of the banjo I'd see if it would work out. That's the way I worked a lot of tunes out."[11]

Talking to banjo players and devotees Béla Fleck and Tony Trischka, Scruggs said of his practice time: "Well, that varied. I was in school. We were on the farm. We'd have to milk cows, feed the mules and slop the hogs, as they call it, and if you had any time left, you'd probably get in a few minutes with the banjo."

Scruggs attended primary school at Boiling Springs, a two-room building with separate privies for boys and girls. With music always on his mind, he occasionally performed at school events, parties, and the like. Shelby resident William Hugh Dover recounted get-togethers where Earl and his friends played music, and Dover, a future radio broadcaster, "announced" the band by speaking into the end of a broom handle. That showed that the young musicians had some notions of show-business success.[12]

Tom Burrus, a Chapel Hill resident whose mother was born the same year as Earl and went to school with him, recalled family stories about the way the young banjo player was initially received in his hometown. "My mom told me a long time ago that when Earl Scruggs would play at talent shows in their school, many of the kids would just giggle at his 'picking' a banjo,'" Burrus said. "I guess in her youth, the banjo was supposed to be strummed."[13]

Throughout Scruggs's life he was to overcome obstacles that could have crushed someone with less fire, ambition, talent, and, perhaps, a smaller share of countervailing good fortune. A Flatt and Scruggs number bore the title "The Good Things Outweigh the Bad." And despite the toll of the Depression, the early death of his father, and the burden of simply helping his family survive, Scruggs plowed ahead, not only to endure, as in Faulkner's phrase, but also to prevail.

$$=\!=\!=$$

Though Scruggs would become likely the most famous native of Cleveland County, the area's formal history takes little recorded notice of farm families such as his. Less than 60 years after the end of the Civil War, the county was known as a powerhouse in North Carolina politics. It reflected changes seen across as the South as the region completed its move into the 20th century.

Some important currents of Southern thought had roots in the county. Preacher and public figure Thomas Dixon, author of *The Clansman*, the book upon which the inflammatory film *The Birth of a Nation* was based, was born in Shelby. In local author Lee B. Weathers's 1956 history of the county, Dixon and his immediate family earn detailed descriptions, including an account of the far-reaching success of his book and of D. W. Griffith's vastly popular movie adaptation.

Weathers cited the "best citizens" of the town as leaders of the Reconstruction-era Ku Klux Klan and described Weathers's own inability to pass up the chance of witnessing a lynching in downtown Shelby. He noted that the Klan eventually outlived what he considered its usefulness as a means of enforcing punishment for crimes and was abandoned by community leaders in the 1870s.

Mind of the South author W. J. Cash, born in nearby Gaffney, South Carolina, spent considerable time in Cleveland County, editing the *Cleveland Press* and writing portions of his most famous work in Boiling Springs. Cash cast a devoted, yet scathing, eye on the South, criticizing more romantic views of its past. He came out strongly against the pro-Klan sentiments expressed by Dixon and others. Both writers are buried in the same Shelby cemetery.

Emerging from this background of strong opinions, Earl Scruggs would later cause occasional moments of controversy because of his political beliefs. He took part in a 1969 demonstration against the Vietnam War, playing "Foggy Mountain Breakdown" and other tunes at the Washington Monument. He collaborated with artists such as Bob Dylan and Joan Baez who were anathema to many conservatives. He spoke out against the Vietnam War but otherwise rarely took overtly political stances.

During the 1930s and '40s, years of change in Cleveland County, Scruggs concentrated on gathering strands of music, some from within his own family, some in the community, and some via radio and records. During the same period, he melded those sounds into a new banjo-picking style.

Musicians and fans have debated for decades whether Scruggs's style was a genuine leap forward or simply a continuation of music he had heard growing up. His part of the world, the piedmont districts of North and

South Carolina, was already home to a distinctive tradition of three-finger banjo picking. In later years, Scruggs was to acknowledge musicians such as Smith Hammett, Rex Brooks, Fisher Hendley, and Snuffy Jenkins as pickers who were playing the banjo when he was still in the region. All used two right-hand fingers and thumb to play with an arpeggiated lilt. But none achieved the strings of "rolls" that Scruggs did, in the flowing picking style that came to bear his name.

3

THE PIEDMONT'S
RICH MUSICAL SOIL

It's about a fifty-mile drive from Shelby to Spartanburg, South Carolina, a trip that touched both poles of a notable acoustic music region in the 20th century's first decades. Earl Scruggs was to make the area famous for its three-finger banjo-picking style, and in accomplishing that he built on rich, varied traditions.

Stringed instruments such as the banjo, fiddle, guitar, and mandolin could be relatively inexpensive in those years, making home entertainment and local performance accessible to lower-income families. After borrowing family instruments for a few years, Scruggs bought his first banjo for $10.95. Stringed instruments were available through mail order or sometimes in the back of small-town furniture stores.

Some folks in North Carolina, mostly farther west, still made banjos out of gourds and without frets, in the style of the African instruments that came to the South from West Africa in the 18th century. Many players used some version of the style called down-picking, in which a player brushes the strings downward with fingernails of the right hand. The technique also calls for the thumb to hit a short drone string in a rhythmic contrast that can get quite complicated. That style, too, was an African holdover.

Rural musicians—in bands and as soloists—played at parties, school events, restaurants, community days, fund-raisers, gospel concerts, "peashellings," and roll-the-rug-back square dances. The Scruggses attended some of these. Young Scruggs got to hear the styles of musicians from outside the region when the family eventually bought a record player and a radio.

At least five musicians—Charlie Poole, Snuffy Jenkins, Fisher Hendley, Smith Hammett, and Mack Woolbright—generally emerge in discussions of possible influences on Scruggs's playing. These players worked in a style in which the thumb picked downward and one or two right-hand fingers plucked up. Some authorities have attributed this approach to the popular sound of the singer, performer, and banjo player Charlie Poole, based north and east of Shelby in what is now Eden, North Carolina. All seem to have contributed in some fashion to Scruggs's playing and performance style, but no single picker stands out as an overriding role model.

═══

Poole, born in 1892, became a defining figure of old-time music based on his vocal and instrumental skills and outsized personality. He played a three-finger style with great precision and accuracy. This style seemed to have derived from the playing of "classic banjo" proponents such as Fred Van Eps. Poole's playing, as well as his voluble singing, was designed to fit seamlessly in the interwoven sound of his band, the North Carolina Ramblers.

"Poole's style was not meant for solo banjo, but blended banjo, fiddle and guitar to create a raggy but controlled sound very different from most other old-time music," musician and old-timey authority Pete Peterson wrote.[1]

Personally, Poole also epitomized a rambling, rough-edged lifestyle, including episodes of violence that would remain linked to old-time music and bluegrass for many decades.

He enjoyed a major hit with his 1925 recording "Don't Let Your Deal Go Down," a tune that later became a bluegrass standard as played by Flatt and Scruggs. He served as a model of a "name" star of string-band music during the years when radio and records became strong forces in the development of new styles. Much of his repertoire was to reemerge in bluegrass, but it was the presence of a five-string banjo played with three fingers that lived on in the new music, not Poole's individual approach to the instrument.

Snuffy Jenkins, born October 27, 1908, was likely the next banjo player to achieve regional prominence using a three-finger approach. No less an authority than Scruggs's contemporary Don Reno gave Jenkins credit for creating the three-finger style and teaching it to Reno. Bill Monroe also attributed what became known as "Scruggs style" to Jenkins. Mountain music performer Ralph Stanley also credited Snuffy and his nephew Hoke Jenkins as his sources for developing a three-finger approach, although Stanley's sound much more closely resembles Scruggs's. These players' opinions, though worth consideration, reflect individual perspectives and competitive biases and aren't widely held.

One of teenage Earl's favorite bands, Byron Parker and His Mountaineers, with Jenkins on banjo, performed on radio station WIS in Columbia, South Carolina, but he often couldn't stay in the house to hear them, not if it was time to go back to work.

"I heard Snuffy," Scruggs said. "I used to hear him on the radio, but not as much as I wanted to hear him, because our work schedule drove us. Soon as we got through with breakfast, we had to see that the mules had something for breakfast.

"And we'd plow till eleven-thirty. Mama had an old bell and rang it, and we'd go home and eat—we called it dinner then, it's lunch now—and cool off. We'd always leave to go back to the field at one o'clock. Well, Snuffy and them came on at one. He sure did, one to one-fifteen."

According to researcher and 78 rpm collector Marshall Wyatt, Scruggs was likely recalling the period around 1938–1940, when both Hendley and Jenkins were heard over station WIS.

"Snuffy was raised not a long ways from me, but Snuffy's a right smart older than me, about 12, 15 years older than me, and he started young in radio," Scruggs said.[2]

Jenkins played widely around the Carolina piedmont, often with his brother Verl. The timing makes it likely that his playing style was among the first heard by Scruggs.

Jenkins typically used what's called a forward roll, in which the thumb, middle, and index finger of the right hand pick the banjo strings in succession. For a musician playing mostly in groups of sixteenth notes, that could lead to getting stuck after playing two thumb-index-middle sequences of three notes each, making up six sixteenth notes with another 10 to go. To release the three-finger style from these periodic interruptions, another figure of some kind was needed to fill the remaining space.

The banjo picker and historian Jim Mills discussed roll patterns one day in 2013 at his house not far from Raleigh, where he keeps a large showroom filled with historically significant banjos and memorabilia.

"Earl'd be the first to tell you he had people playing the three-finger style in his area when he was a child, but clearly he perfected it," Mills said. "He straightened out the roll that was a jerky, jumpy kind of thing. What Earl could do that no one else before him, to my knowledge, could do, and do it on a regular basis, and do it on every song consistently, was to straighten out the timing on a three-finger banjo roll.

"And the way he did that was, he could alternate his roll forward or backward. Any time at his will, he could change that. Where guys like Snuffy Jenkins played more or less of a forward roll straight through, and then they would stop and do a pinch to create a timing jump, or a stop, or a change, Earl could stop and do a forward or a backward roll to make it come out right timing-wise. It was smooth and it was very flowing."[3]

Jenkins continued to play late in life. I was fortunate to see his performance in June 1988 at a medicine-show festival in Red Boiling Springs, Tennessee. His engaging playing heard in person and on recordings was strikingly direct and rhythmic, with clear elements of three-finger patterns that might well have influenced Scruggs. But his sound lacked the smoothness and overwhelming drive that Scruggs pioneered.

"I don't claim to have taught Earl or Don [Reno], either one, anything," Jenkins said in 1977. "It's got to be born in you, I think. You got it or you don't have it. But I was always willing to teach anyone anything. I could do it and let them pick it up in a short time."[4]

Jenkins died in 1990.

Like Poole, Fisher Hendley played a style that derived more directly from the classic banjo style than from the approach that would emerge as Scruggs's signature. Hendley, born in 1891, had a long career in radio and personal appearances and cultivated a respectable, high-toned image while becoming an enduring influence on music in the piedmont.

In 1933, Hendley in his role of musical statesman announced an ambitious program to hold a championship fiddle contest in every county in North Carolina. These contests were to culminate in a statewide contest with total cash prizes of $1,000.[5] In later years, he changed with the times and recorded pop-leaning material such as Floyd Tillman's "It Makes No Difference."

Decades later, Scruggs remembered that Hendley had "a kind of a Western type band. The reason I say Western, he had accordion in the band. He had a fiddle player; his name was Sam Poplin."

"He had the Aristocratic Pigs [band] and I mentioned that name one time and somebody got offended; I think it was [longtime Opry manager] Ott Devine. Somebody at the Grand Ole Opry thought I was making fun of them, calling 'em Pigs, but that's what they said they were. And their slogan, 'The finest meats you could buy,' was because they come from Aristocratic Pigs."

Hendley may have helped Scruggs build a mental image of what it was like to be a professional entertainer, but his playing doesn't appear to have been a crucial influence.

However, Hendley did have a notable banjo, a Gibson Mastertone that he had bought new. It traveled through several famous players' hands before it wound up in Earl's. In a quirk of history, Scruggs wrote and first recorded "Foggy Mountain Breakdown" on that instrument.

═══

As in his comments on Jenkins, Scruggs sometimes varied the details of his exposure to the music of his predecessors in the three-finger style. During a 2007 interview, son Gary Scruggs was on hand and occasionally prompted Earl, as Louise Scruggs had done during previous interviews. Earl Scruggs recounted the time he went on a family visit to his uncle Sid Ruppe's house and encountered Mack Woolbright, a fine banjoist who was blind.

"I saw him when I was four or five years old," Scruggs said. "He was at my Uncle Sid's, my mama's brother, who lived over near the South Carolina line, which was when we lived 10, 15 miles just inside the North Carolina line. I went over to Uncle Sid's one weekend, and he had Mack Woolbright visiting with him."

According to newspaper accounts, Woolbright, born about 1891 in South Carolina, stayed busy around the region, promoting his recordings, playing as a soloist, teaching students on several different instruments and leading bands, including Woolbright's Serenaders.

"He was blind, the first blind man I had ever seen," Scruggs said. "And they had a recording of him, seemed like Mack Woolbright and Charlie Parker, but I may be wrong on the other guy that was on that record. And I think they recorded 'The Man Who Wrote Home Sweet Home Never Was a Married Man.' And they played that while he was there and I was just sitting on the floor and looking at him."

Scruggs had the name of the record and the artists right. Woolbright's banjo was featured on the song, the raucous tale of a man whose evil-minded wife beat him with a frying pan. His partner on the record, Charlie Parker, had died not long after the record was issued in 1928.

Young Earl clearly had an active mind and an eye for unusual situations, going outside his own perspective to examine how Woolbright felt.

"I thought, what in the world . . . is going through his mind, sitting there hearing him sing the song with the other guy who was dead, you know? That guy just confused the s—t out of me, a little kid."

Banjo player and historian Bob Carlin has done extensive research into the musicians who are often mentioned as influencing Scruggs. According to Carlin's research, Charlie Parker, not to be confused with the legendary jazz saxophonist, died in 1931, which would put Earl at 6 or 7 years old at the time of the encounter.

Scruggs had said in earlier interviews that he was particularly impressed with Woolbright's use of a G7 chord in C tuning, a captivating sound to his young ears.

"Well, that's the first time I had ever heard that G7 thing, and played in C," Scruggs said. "And I thought that G7 was the prettiest chord I'd ever heard on the banjo."

There is direct evidence of Woolbright's influence on Scruggs. The rolling three-finger style Woolbright played on "The Man Who Wrote Home Sweet Home Never Was a Married Man" was reflected in later years in Scruggs's showcase version of "Home Sweet Home."

Another banjo player Scruggs mentioned as an influence was Smith Hammett, who was born in 1887 in South Carolina and died on February 1, 1930, when Scruggs was barely six years old. In an incident related by Lula Scruggs that stayed rooted in Earl's mind for many decades, Smith Hammett died in wintertime, unexpectedly and early in life.

"He was married to my mother's cousin," Scruggs said in 2007. "And Smith got killed when I was about four or five years old.[6]

"He farmed and I think he saved all his drinking 'til he got the farm about gathered in, in the wintertime, and he'd stay on a drunk. That's the way I remember Mama talking about it. And he was high-strung, and he rented from a guy that had just an old rural store. Sold general junk, stuff that farmers need, you know, coffee, soda and salt, pepper, stuff like that, and I don't know what else, in the store.

"But Smith was there, they said. And the store was kind of shotgun-built, it was longer than it was wide, you know? And the counter over there, and behind the counter was the candy and stuff.

"It was wintertime, I reckon. Anyway, the old potbelly stove was still up, might've left it up year-round, I don't know. He had an old dog laying back there, and Smith stumbled around in the room there, and stepped on the dog. You know they're gonna holler when you do that, and it made Smith mad. And he was gonna kill the dog.

"And the store man went, 'Sir, think nothing about the dog, it just hollered 'cause you stepped on it,' or whatever he said, and then Hammett came at him. I don't know what kind of temper you'd call it, that and the lick alcohol added in, and just had no sense.

"And Hammett was coming at him with that poking iron and this guy had a 12-gauge shotgun and he just shot the whole side of Hammett's face off, killed him right there in the store. He'd killed him, or Smith would've killed him."

The story Lula Scruggs told Earl about Hammett reflected random violence of the sort that might have been seen in country crossroads or in big-city mobs, turning up both in real life and later sensationalized in movies like *Bonnie and Clyde*. Scruggs's version showed that, despite his taciturn reputation, he could weave a spell in conversation as well as on the banjo.

Hammett was just shy of 43 years old when he died, his rippling banjo style gone for good. Contemporary accounts mostly echo the story of

Hammett's death that his mother told Scruggs. The newspapers said the storeowner, Charles Godfrey, killed Hammett in self-defense at Godfrey's store in the rural Cherokee Church community. Godfrey was a friend of Hammett's, according to the Gaffney paper. But Hammett was "under the influence of alcohol," and the slaying was found to be justifiable, just as Lula Scruggs had told Earl.[7]

"So did you get to hear him play before he got killed?" I asked him.

Said Scruggs, "I guess I did, but I can't remember what he sounded like."

However, as mentioned, Scruggs gave different accounts on different occasions. In 1973, he told an interviewer a story about adapting the three-finger roll. The account stood out for its detail and depiction of the Scruggs home life.

"I went in and told my mother I could play like Smith Hammett," Scruggs said. "She always knew I liked music so much and never did scold me for making noise or anything. I don't know how she put up with all that noise.

"Actually, I could do the finger roll that I do now, but it didn't sound exactly like Smith. . . . So I decided to put my own thoughts in it and that's how I came up with the style that I now play."[8]

═══

A story in a 1985 community history, "Roots of Rutherford," offers a fascinating, if not readily verifiable, glimpse of the possible origins of Hammett's style. A man named Lewis Jolley told the story to Ben Humphries, a booster of the region's music:

"Smith was a well-known clawhammer banjo picker at the time, during the 'teens and 'twenties. One day a Black man came to the Flint Hill School playing a three-finger picking style on the banjo.

"Smith asked George Elam Scruggs if he could play that lick on the banjo. George replied, 'No, I don't believe I can.' Smith said, 'I can't either, but I will.' Within two to three weeks he was playing that three-finger style. He perfected it and taught many people how to play it."[9]

There's no other available evidence that the piedmont three-finger style had its roots in an African American musician's presence in the area. But it's a compelling legend, if that's what it is, right down to the presence of George Elam Scruggs on the scene.

═══

Through the years, fans, pickers, and journalists have tried to pin down exact influences for Scruggs's individual style. At age 83, while acknowledging he had heard, or heard of, players like Jenkins, Hammett and Woolbright, he maintained that the invention was his own. It was rare for him even to hear another musician, he said.

"There just wasn't a lot of people lived close to us, and we didn't have a car, we just had a mule and buggy, so we didn't go much ourselves or nothing," Scruggs said. "Lived on the farm. We had hogs and cows and stuff to see after, so I'd have to be there for milking every night, and milking in the morning."

I asked him: "So when you started playing your own style at 10 or 11, then you had not heard anybody play that way before?"

He responded: "No, no. And I'd been playing with just thumb and finger."

That takes the story back to the farm in Flint Hill. Most of all, in historical terms, the old house was the scene of the creation story that Scruggs often related. He was practicing an old tune, "Reuben," in a two-finger style, over and over. All of a sudden, he said, he was playing the bluesy railroad tune in a three-finger style that he had been hearing in his head.

"You've sat in a daydream like, and be picking and not even noticing what you're doing?" Scruggs said at his home in 1998. "That was the mode I was in . . .

"And I was sitting in the, like we'd call this a front room, where somebody'd come in and you've got the couch big enough for everybody to sit around like we are and talk, and bring 'em in here.

"I was in there by myself one day playing this tune called 'Reuben' that I still play, in D tuning. And all of a sudden I had this roll that I still do going. And Horace, my brother, said I came out of the room, said, 'I got it! I got it!' He said that's what I was saying. I don't know what I had, thought I had, but anyway, I played that one tune the rest of the week."

≡≡≡

Years later, Brother Horace recalled Earl's reaction to his discovery.

"Boy, he sounded good," Horace told writer Joe DePriest. "He was all smiles, that's for sure. I knew it was an important jump in his music. But I didn't know how important."[10]

But Earl Scruggs also had to put up with the kind of jealous scrutiny that often falls upon innovators. Scruggs remembered older brother Junie, himself a notable banjo player, walking up the path to the Flint Hill house, cocking his head and listening as the young banjoist rolled through "Reuben" over and again.

"Is that all you can do?" asked Junie, who no longer lived at the family home.

The question startled young Scruggs. He had played only "Reuben," hundreds of times, in the new style, and immediately wondered whether his brother might be right. Was the three-finger roll a sort of trick that only worked for one song?

But he found that the new style worked in other tunings, keys, tempos, and even time signatures. And he heard it as his own style, he said in 1972.

"It didn't sound like Smith Hammett and Snuffy and Junie," he said. "Later on it seemed to turn out to be a little more versatile than their style. I've had a chance to play so many different tunes from what they played. They had just a very few tunes, like 'Cripple Creek' and 'Reuben,' 'Sally Goodwin' and a few tunes like that is all they played back then."[11]

Given the adventurous nature of musicians, another banjo player could have come along to move the instrument into different tunes and different styles. But Scruggs took the lead. His sound arose from the area's rich musical lore, from the new popular music in the air, and from a deep determination to find something different and exciting to play.

4

EARLY PROFESSIONAL DAYS

If 11-year-old Earl Scruggs had achieved his breakthrough on an instrument other than the banjo, in a larger place than his Flint Hill front room, he might have arrived much sooner on the national stage. Instead, it took about a decade for Scruggs to move on from front-porch and small-town music sessions, to regional radio, then to the nationally heard WSM Grand Ole Opry broadcast.

Young Earl initially picked in a two-finger style of the day, at family gatherings, with neighborhood groups and at fiddle contests, wherever he could practice his growing skills in front of people.

By age 6, he took his first steps in a more professional direction. He went with his family to play on radio station WSPA in Spartanburg, in his best Sunday clothes and with slicked-back hair.[1]

In Depression-era Flint Hill, Earl continued to attend nearby Boiling Springs High School and to pull his weight on the farm. People around Cleveland County remembered young Earl's playing from those days, well into the 21st century. Brooks Piercy was Earl's teacher at the high school in Boiling Springs as well as his accomplice on one of his first road trips, to a stringed-instrument contest in nearby Casar in 1938. (According to the *North Carolina Gazetteer*, the town had intended to take the name of the Roman emperor

Julius Caesar, but fell victim to a spelling error.) "Of course we won the thing, but they wouldn't let Earl stop playing," Piercy said when in his '90s.[2]

Scruggs's daily work was so time-consuming that he began looking for a way to support himself and his family by other means.

"All it amounted to in those days was just trying to play with whatever groups I could get with and working as many places as possible," he said. "I just enjoyed—even back then—different atmospheres and different locations."[3]

As mentioned, Earl sometimes played at one of Cleveland County's fish camps, an informal kind of spot that *Charlotte Observer* reporter Joe De-Priest described as "a screened-in shack with a few picnic tables," where diners could get fresh-caught catfish, slaw, and other dishes. Scruggs told DePriest that he used to walk from his house with his brother to play at Ollie Moore's fish camp on the Broad River, some three miles below Boiling Springs.[4]

"We'd put on clean overalls and work shirts and make about a nickel apiece," Horace Scruggs said.[5]

Late in life, Earl Scruggs recalled an idyllic scene by the river, with wooden shutters propped open, kerosene lamps glowing, people dancing, and a piedmont breeze keeping everyone comfortable.

"It was a pretty scene, hearing the Broad River running, and it was cool down there on a hot summer night," he said.[6]

As Earl grew, hard times on the farm led to his taking a job at a mill in Shelby. Trish Camp, daughter of Earl's friend and eventual picking partner Grady Wilkie, has heard stories about Scruggs all her life. Camp said that her father, who worked at Lily Mills in Shelby, was friends with Lula, Earl's mother. Lula visited Wilkie to ask whether he could "get Earl on" at the thread mill, that is, see that he was hired to a full-time, cash-money job.

"We're about on starvation and we need some help if you can get him on," Camp said, as she recalled the words of Lula Scruggs's plea.[7]

And Wilkie did. He reached out to young Earl, got him a job at the mill, and had him stay with the family.

"Mom and Dad just lived right up the street from the mill, on Morton Street," Camp said. "They would all walk to work together every day."

Even at the thread mill, Scruggs found opportunities to work on his craft, picking with Wilkie in the backseat of Earl's Chevy during breaks.

"He'd play guitar and I'd play banjo until they'd motion us to come back into the mill," Scruggs said. "That's when I finally realized that what I was doing was of interest to other people. They'd stand around and watch us pick."

"One of them hadn't heard nothing like that before, and he took his hat off, threw it on the ground and said, 'Hot damn!' That's the only time I've run into a guy that when he got excited would throw his hat down and dance on it. . . . That's hard on a hat."[8]

———

As Scruggs continued to encounter the world outside the farm, he started pondering the idea that music might be more than his private obsession: It might become his job. In 1941, he did a stint with Paul Carpenter and the Orange Blossom Hillbillies, picking along with his buddy Wilkie and guitarists Carpenter, Junior Wiseman, and Charles Hopper. One January they played at the opening of Bridges Amoco service station near Lattimore, North Carolina.

Scruggs played an early radio stint with the Gastonia-based Carolina Wildcats band and then encountered a brother team who had climbed higher up the show-business ladder. His first professional job came playing dates with Zeke, Wiley, and George Morris. Many sources, probably relying on Earl Scruggs's own banjo book, give 1939 as the year when he joined the Morris Brothers. For several reasons, that date is likely inaccurate.

Earl was only 15 in 1939 and still in high school in Boiling Springs. But more significantly, several sources say he replaced banjo player Hoke Jenkins, Snuffy Jenkins's nephew, who was going into the service. According to Army records, Hoke Jenkins was inducted in January 1941.

The 1940 census shows Earl Scruggs still living at home in Flint Hill. Most North Carolina high schools were in the process from going from an 11-year schedule to one that specified graduation after 12 years. That means Scruggs probably graduated in spring 1941.

Earl likely went to work with the Morrises in 1941 or possibly early 1942, as the brothers said there was a gap between Jenkins's leaving and their hiring Earl.

The Morrises, best known for their version of the eventual Flatt and Scruggs favorite "Salty Dog Blues," had been working as bandleaders and separately as side musicians in the network of radio stations that kept pickers busy in North and South Carolina. Wiley Morris told journalist Wayne Erbsen about the night Scruggs and his mill friend Grady Wilkie showed up at a date in Chesney, South Carolina.

"They had both driven up to Chesney in a model A Ford coupe, and both were wearing blue shirts and overalls," Morris said. "Grady said, 'I got a guy out here I wish you boys would listen to on the five-string banjo.' Well, we were needing one at the time because Hoke Jenkins had been called into the service, so I said, 'Bring him in here. Let's tune him up and hear how he sounds.'

"So Earl came in and tuned his banjo to my guitar, and he could play as good that night as he can now, if not better. He was just shaky and nervous then. He's always been nervous and I'd have thought he'd have missed everything on the banjo, but he didn't miss a string. So we hired him that night and paid him 20 dollars a week."

Jesse McReynolds, of the highly regarded brother team Jim & Jesse, remembered the Morris Brothers as a colorful act with raucous overtones.[9]

"They couldn't get along playing for fighting together," McReynolds said. "A lot of their show was fighting on stage."

Like most hillbilly acts of the day, the Morris Brothers included lots of comedy in their performances, including blackface and cross-dressing routines. It is not known what role, if any, Scruggs played in the Morris Brothers' hijinks, although he later described his attempts at comedy as mostly unsuccessful. Scruggs spent about eight months with the Morris Brothers, according to Wiley, then returned to Cleveland County and received his draft notice in 1942.

Because his father had died, Scruggs got a deferment to stay out of the Army and support his mother. As World War II neared an end, Scruggs continued to work in the textile mill and then hooked up in 1945 with another regional act, Lost John Miller and his Allied Kentuckians, based in Knoxville. Jim Mills, who zealously collects anything associated with Scruggs, once took Scruggs a picture of Miller's band circa 1945, more than 40 years later.[10]

"They never took a picture with Earl in the band," Mills said. "He was only in the band about six months."

Scruggs recalled Miller fondly, Mills said, and could still name all the Allied Kentuckians. But in the day, the band couldn't get past Miller's personal situation.

"The main problem with the band was his wife," Mills said Scruggs told him. "She just nagged the hell out of him all the time and he gave it up. That's when Jim Shumate called me and said, 'Hey, why don't you try out with Bill Monroe?'"

By 1946, Miller was back on the road with a fresh batch of Allied Kentuckians, but he never regained the place in history that came from his hiring Earl Scruggs.

Many years later, in an article that accompanied his National Heritage Fellowship from the National Endowment for the Arts in 1989, Scruggs offered a glimpse of the struggle he went through in deciding to commit to music. After all, he was a smart, capable young man with beautiful handwriting, the son of an accountant and a church organist, educated in school and on the land. He could have done plenty of things other than pick the banjo.

The NEA essay gets deeper into Scruggs's thoughts during that time than almost any other interview:

"The music business was, he said, 'like looking into a dark room,' and after playing with a few local bands, he was 'forced to weigh carefully whether it would be stable or not.' As he began to refine his three-finger picking technique, he wasn't sure whether he was going in the right direction with his music. 'I wasn't happy about what I was doing,' he said, 'but I didn't know what to do about it.'"[11]

In his early twenties, Scruggs had played everywhere the opportunity arose since his preteen years but remained mostly unknown outside his original stomping grounds. However, Scruggs was about to be offered as much work as he could handle, playing in country music's big leagues.

5

JOINING BILL MONROE

The backstage area at the Ryman Auditorium in Nashville, where the Opry held sway in the 1940s, was an important crossroads in the evolving map of country music. The Ryman, extensively renovated in recent years, was then a warren of tiny dressing rooms and wood-walled corridors, where old-time string bands mingled with solo stars such as Roy Acuff and smooth gospel groups like the Oak Ridge Quartet, later the Oak Ridge Boys. Musicians and visitors wandered freely, sometimes crowding the dressing rooms of the former gospel tabernacle with off-the-cuff picking sessions.

Scruggs's talent had previously won him time on the radio when he traveled from Knoxville to appear on WSM in Nashville with Lost John Miller and the Allied Kentuckians. But when his friend Jim Shumate arranged an audition with Opry star Bill Monroe, the moment stood out like Jimmy Stewart's address to Congress in *Mr. Smith Goes to Washington* or farm-girl Dorothy's arrival in the Technicolor landscape of Oz. A rural citizen was getting a good shot at glory.

After Scruggs rose from working as a regional side musician to being a key band member for Monroe, the young picker captivated listeners, created a tune that was a close forerunner of "Foggy Mountain Breakdown," and began to build his own brand as Earl Scruggs. His musical development had largely taken place in North Carolina, but the career he built in Nashville would transport his music, initially throughout the region and eventually the world.

———

At 34, Bill Monroe had starred on the powerful Opry radio show since 1939. He succeeded there after parting ways with duet partner and brother Charlie in 1938. As a bandleader, Monroe had been building a broad following with a diverse group of songs such as "Kentucky Waltz" and "Mule Skinner Blues." Monroe's music with his Blue Grass Boys band featured high-pitched singing and inventive harmonizing. It also made a trademark out of lightning-fast, often improvised picking that grew ever more intense after Scruggs joined.

Monroe, born September 13, 1911, had employed a series of musicians, including guitarist-vocalist Clyde Moody, accordionist Wilene (Sally Ann) Forrester and banjo player David (Stringbean) Akeman. He was searching for a group that could match the sound his complicated musical soul had conceived. Like Scruggs, Monroe had come from a farm region and always kept in mind an audience of country people.

Radio was in its early stages as Monroe grew up, so he learned about music first from live fiddling, guitar playing, and harmony singing, mostly in his home community of Rosine, Kentucky. More specifically, he cited elements such as Holiness church singing, his mother Malissa's fiddling, the sentimental songs and country tunes of the day, the blues played by African American guitarist Arnold Schultz and the old-time fiddling of his Uncle Pen Vandiver.

Also like Scruggs, Monroe started work in music early, riding a mule to back up Vandiver's fiddling at square dances when he was 12 or 13.[1] With his brother Charlie and as a bandleader, Monroe had enjoyed a well-traveled career before he met Scruggs, logging radio time in Illinois, Iowa, South Carolina, North Carolina, and Arkansas before securing his spot at the Grand Ole Opry. The Monroe Brothers also had a notable record career on Bluebird Records before splitting up in Raleigh, where they had spent several years on WPTF.

On December 8, 1945, a little more than three months after the end of World War II, Scruggs made his first Opry appearance in Monroe's band.

Several anecdotes have persisted about the audition that led to Scruggs's job with Monroe. In one, guitaristo-vocalist Lester Flatt, already with the Blue Grass Boys, suggested to Monroe that Scruggs could put his banjo back in the case, because Flatt didn't particularly want the instrument in the band. Flatt, who became Scruggs's co-bandleader a few years later, changed his tune when he heard Scruggs play. After that, he suggested hiring the banjo player at any cost.

Another story points to how closely people linked banjo playing and humor in that era. Scruggs often quoted the great banjoist and entertainer Uncle Dave Macon, who called Scruggs "Ernest" in a bit of whimsy. "Ernest, you pick good in a band, but you ain't a damn bit funny," Macon said, according to Scruggs.[2]

Macon wasn't merely cracking wise, given the popularity of banjo-playing comedians such as Snuffy Jenkins, Bashful Brother Oswald, and Akeman. But Scruggs's powerful talent, even without a comedic side, helped fortify Monroe's music-first presentation.

Scruggs recalled years later that he tried his best to come up with a shtick, but it only distracted him from playing his best. "Well, I used to just try to see if there was some kind of routine I wanted to do as being a comedian," he told "Fresh Air" interviewer Terry Gross in 2003. "But all my interest was just in picking. Not only tunes, but songs behind the singers; not only the lead part, but doing a backup. You know what I mean by backup?" Gross murmured a response.

Said Scruggs, "It's playing an alto or something to support the singer. So, that's where my interest was, not just as a lead picker with the banjo but also a supporter with the banjo."

Indeed, Scruggs's tasteful backup playing—harmonizing or ornamenting a tune that was sung or played by another band member—can be heard beginning with his recordings with Monroe. Other musicians and listeners prized this skill highly. Whatever he played behind the lead singer or soloist seemed to make the vocal emerge even more brightly. His skill in playing backup could be compared to that of a harpsichordist in the Baroque era, improvising over a figured or designated bass line. This approach also emphasized Scruggs's instincts as a whole musician, making a clear statement while keeping his ears tuned to the ensemble sound.

≡

When Scruggs started work with Monroe, he produced such a hard-hitting sound that audiences cheered for him like bettors at a prizefight, a reaction that can be heard on live recordings of the Opry.

"When I first got here," Scruggs said, "Uncle Dave Macon was the big star, and he was a typical banjo player. He might play a little lick, but he used it more as a simple, rhythmic accompaniment.

"I made it a lead instrument. At the time there weren't any other pickers like me, so it was all brand new. This new music was faster than what had come before, and that fit me because I played really well on up-tempo tunes."[3]

The idea of a banjo as a lead instrument—to play hot improvised solos, as the fiddle and mandolin had been doing in the Blue Grass Boys—was indeed brand new in country music, though Bob Wills and other Western swing musicians were already featuring "takeoff" passages on fiddle, steel, and guitar. Indeed, Scruggs happened to join Monroe during a time when musical experimentation and transformation were leaping across the musical spectrum. The relative ease of the postwar, automobile-powered economy, along with the growing power of radio, records, and movies, laid almost infinite choices before musicians and audiences.

The major bluegrass figure Mac Wiseman, later a guitarist and singer for Monroe, told me that Monroe didn't know exactly where his music was headed in those early years. Scruggs's fire ignited the kindling that Monroe had spent more than six years gathering, Wiseman said.

"I don't think to this day he set out with a theory or a way to go," he said of Monroe. "He was just doing his thing and doing it with a drive he couldn't do with Charlie [Monroe]. In his first bands, he didn't have a sense of direction. He didn't say, 'I am going to create bluegrass music.' I give him credit for sticking to his guns. As far as being a founding genius, he did it, but without any intention. He had that drive."

In Earl Scruggs, Wiseman said, the Blue Grass Boys gained "just the thing that Monroe needed to feed off."[4]

≡

The musical interactions among this band's members between 1945 and 1948 remain much discussed 70 years later. At the center of this history lies the question: What is bluegrass, and who really got it started?

Bluegrass, generally, is an acoustic music, using strong, often high-pitched lead and harmony singing, backed with banjo, fiddle, mandolin, upright bass, and guitar played in highly accomplished versions of tradition-based styles. As the style that would become bluegrass developed, Monroe was combining elements from contemporary country music, blues, traditional fiddling, Celtic sounds, and the Holiness church singing of his youth. As opposed to the ensemble sound of most of the string-band music that preceded it, bluegrass allowed individual lead singers and instrumentalists to shine.

"I think when Earl came into it, Bill *was* the band, he was the star," modern-day banjo star Béla Fleck said. "He (Monroe) was used to being Mr. Somebody. The band members didn't find him very much fun to be around."[5]

                    ≡

However cantankerous and self-absorbed Monroe may have been at times, he also had an unflagging drive to make his music as powerful as possible. And that meant featuring Earl Scruggs as a Blue Grass Boy.

Scruggs landed in a Nashville that wasn't yet Music City but was already a magnet for skilled musicians. Country music entertainers also performed, recorded, and appeared on radio out of California, Texas, the Midwest, the Carolinas, and the Washington, D.C., area, among other places. But WSM-AM (650), the Opry's radio home, represented a prominent place in the music industry, an influential stage from which Scruggs could be heard.

Wiley Morris said Scruggs's tryout while still in his teens showed that he was already playing at a high level. Bill Monroe would later claim that Scruggs had come to the Blue Grass Boys with limited skills. But the general consensus and recorded performances agree that Scruggs's playing elevated Monroe's already driving sound to a pulse-quickening new level. Scruggs described the element he added as "punch."

"It just seemed to me like an energy-type music," Scruggs said. "You've got to punch it to make it jibe . . . it's like Western [music] just has a certain pace to it and it don't seem like it needs a punch to it.

"But what we now call bluegrass seemed to me like it just needs a punch to give it a little energy."

Even as a younger, less experienced musician than Monroe, Scruggs had a notion that startling things could happen if he drove the already energy-cranked mandolin man to greater heights.

"That one man, I sensed way back then that if you wanted to hear him pick really good, push him a little bit," Scruggs told me. "The more you pushed him or crowded him, the better he would play. I think everybody has some of that built in.

"If you love music and someone is really laying in with you, it makes you dig deeper."[6]

Another feature of the new music introduced by Monroe was the use of higher-pitched keys than those used in old-time music. Flatt and Scruggs used capos, clamps that attach to an instrument's neck to make its pitch higher, and chords easier to play in unconventional keys. (Scruggs even pioneered the use of a fifth-string capo, which he made from a hairpin driven into the banjo's fingerboard.) But Monroe, fiddler Chubby Wise, and bassist Cedric Rainwater had to play in the more difficult keys, often so that Monroe's high tenor would appear to its best advantage.

"Back in the early days of bluegrass music," Monroe said, "when I started on the Grand Ole Opry, the people that played there, they played in G, C, and D. Or they played in D, or played in G, or C. But they didn't go up and play in B flat or B natural or E minor or anything like that. Not 'til the Blue Grass Boys started there."[7]

Monroe was a complex, often prickly man, and unpredictable. It sometimes seemed as though he made improbable statements just to get a strong reaction. Then he'd retreat to facts nearer to the literal truth. In a 1986 interview with the notable banjo pickers and scholars Tony Trischka and Pete Wernick, Monroe insisted that Snuffy Jenkins had been the originator of the three-finger banjo style. But then he gave Scruggs something of his due, before maintaining that it was bluegrass that completed Earl Scruggs, not the other way around. He cited as an example Scruggs's approach to the popular up-tempo tune "Molly and Tenbrooks," about a Kentucky horse race.

"His way of playin' it was fine, you see," Monroe said. "It done a lot for 'Molly and Tenbrooks.' That number done a lot for fiddle playin', and a good fiddler done a lot for the number, too. But the numbers that I come with, I knew that they would fit the banjo and it would help the banjo and the banjo would help me."

"The drive that the bluegrass music had helped the five-string banjo. But if I'd have went on back and got the old-time mountain music and played it, the banjo wouldn't never have come out. If it hadn't been for bluegrass, the five-string banjo would have never made it."[8]

It's doubtless true that Scruggs's musical ability and scope got a boost from Monroe's experience and fast-paced tempos. Reflecting a more widely held interpretation, historians Bill C. Malone and Jocelyn Neal described Scruggs's impact on the group: "When Earl Scruggs joined Bill Monroe's Blue Grass Boys in 1945, he brought with him a sensational technique that rejuvenated the five-string banjo, made his own name preeminent among country and folk musicians, and established bluegrass music as a national phenomenon."[9] Said Steve Martin, the musician, actor, and comedian, "It's often said that Earl really defined that sound. Once Earl came in, that's when it coalesced."[10]

Scruggs and Monroe had their differences, but they also shared a bond that continued long after their separation in 1948. They were to play together several times in the '70s and later. At one appearance at his Bean Blossom festival, Monroe praised Scruggs and mentioned a little-known series of shows they did.

"When Earl Scruggs went to work with me on the Grand Ole Opry, he was a single man," Monroe told the audience. "Some of the fellows that worked with me was married, you know, and they would want to go home for Christmas. But Earl would stay right there. He would stay there and he would pick the five-string banjo and I would sing solos and play the guitar behind him. That's been a long, long time ago."

Scruggs interjected, "That's some of the best Christmas I ever had."

Said Monroe, "Oh, it was fine, man."

At the same Bean Blossom show, Scruggs used a card-playing metaphor to express how perfectly Monroe's music suited him when they joined forces at the Opry.

"When I went to work with him in 1945, it was one of the most exciting times of my life," Scruggs told the Bean Blossom crowd. "It really hit my hole card."[11]

Monroe's new songs and interpretations of traditional fiddle tunes, blues, and country tunes were turning out to be a perfect fit with Scruggs's complex three-finger banjo picking and ideas about solos and backup. Although no one was using the term yet, "bluegrass" music was taking a shape that could be defined and replicated. Scruggs-style banjo became key to that definition.

WORKING AS A
BLUE GRASS BOY

By 1945, Bill Monroe had been experimenting with different sounds and instruments, including the jug and accordion, since he split up with brother Charlie in 1938. The fertile post–World War II years saw a reward emerge for Monroe's dogged search. He moved forward with the Blue Grass Boys band and a style of music that worked for fans and for him, personally and commercially.

Lester Flatt, an accomplished guitar picker and singer from Sparta, Tennessee, was a veteran of acts including Charlie Monroe's Kentucky Pardners before he joined Monroe in 1944. Flatt brought mellow vocals, winning stage presence, incisive songwriting, and a trademark guitar style to the Blue Grass Boys, and then to the band with Scruggs.

Born June 19, 1914, Flatt had musical skills and rapport with an audience that merit their own story.

"Lester was the Bing Crosby of the bluegrass world. He didn't cut corners, he sang the whole melody," said Dobro star Jerry Douglas, who brought about a major Flatt and Scruggs revival with his band the Earls of Leicester in 2014.[1]

Flatt, a more experienced entertainer and nearly 10 years older than Scruggs, also helped create a more accessible approach to the evolving bluegrass sound. He presented a smoother vocal style than Monroe's and wrote songs that pictured the rambunctious postwar South as well as old times on the farm.

Scruggs's Tar Heel friend Jim Shumate, who had been key to Scruggs's getting his job with Monroe, left the Blue Grass Boys fiddle slot during the same period. Fiddler Howdy Forrester, who had gone into military service while playing with Monroe in 1942, got his job back, as he was entitled to do when he completed his duty for Uncle Sam. When Scruggs joined, the Blue Grass Boys included Flatt, Forrester, his bassist brother Joe, and the pioneering female accordionist and singer Wilene (Sally Ann) Forrester, Howdy's wife.

The Forresters' joint departure in about March 1946 set the stage for what has become known as the "classic" lineup of Monroe, Flatt, Scruggs, fiddler Chubby Wise, and bassist Howard Watts, using the comedic stage name Cedric Rainwater.

Like Monroe on mandolin and Scruggs on banjo, Wise helped set the standard for bluegrass musicianship, in his case with nimble, hot fiddle playing. This quintet, with occasional changes in lineup, provided much of the core repertoire of bluegrass with tunes such as "Will You Be Loving Another Man," "Molly and Tenbrooks," "Wicked Path of Sin," and "My Little Georgia Rose."

Either Flatt or Monroe, or the two working together, wrote many of the band's tunes. As early commercial singer-songwriters, they paved the way for bluegrass as a field in which the performers often wrote or adapted the songs they recorded.

Flatt wrote some of the most memorable songs of early bluegrass, including "Will You Be Loving Another Man" and "Little Cabin Home on the Hill." When Flatt's songs appeared on record with Monroe's name as cowriter, Scruggs's awareness that there was money in writing songs sparked him to try to get his own name on some copyrights. Side musicians in the hillbilly bands of the day often shared credit for songs they had written in order to get a tune recorded by the bandleader.

Scruggs told me in 2007: "Lester had written some songs and gave Bill half of it to get him to record it. Well, I wrote 'Blue Grass Breakdown' and I thought he'd give me half of it. He didn't give me nothing."[2]

More than 50 years later when Scruggs talked about "Blue Grass Breakdown," the slight still rankled of losing the credit for this tune. "Blue Grass Breakdown," with its ear-catching G to F progression, doesn't have the immediate appeal of "Foggy Mountain Breakdown," but it has a similar drive and intensity. It was recorded in several different takes, with the structure of breaks varying on each. Monroe was to claim its authorship and what he claimed was a key influence on "Foggy Mountain Breakdown." But Scruggs never wavered in his insistence that "Blue Grass Breakdown" was his tune that Monroe had taken from him.

Scruggs educated himself about everything from playing music to learning the entertainment business to, many years later, flying his own airplane. He was young when he came to the Grand Ole Opry but quickly learned both the broad outlines and the fine points of the business. Faced with what he always regarded as the theft of his song "Blue Grass Breakdown," Scruggs never confronted Monroe, who was, after all, his boss.

"No, I thought, 'Well, I was the stupid one, so I won't even try to bring it up,'" he said. "But you know—you can tell it's not his writing. He never did write anything else as close to it anyway, that he played. But I was young and getting a lot of exposure and I didn't create no problems with it."

The musician and historian Pete Kuykendall took the position in an interview that "Blue Grass Breakdown" was Monroe's work, given its resemblance to other Monroe tunes, but his remains a minority view.[3] Curly Seckler, another North Carolina bluegrass pioneer, in 2013 confirmed the broader idea that bandleaders often took credit for songs written by side musicians.

"Back then, if I wrote a song and if they recorded it, they got half. That's the way it was back in them days," said Seckler, who was 93 when interviewed in his home north of Nashville. "Lester's got his name on a bunch of songs I wrote. Back then, whoever recorded it got half; I don't know why it was that way."

Monroe and band recorded "Blue Grass Breakdown" for Columbia on October 27, 1947, at the WBBM-CBS studio in Chicago, during a session that ran from 7:30 p.m. until 10:45 p.m.[4] The released version kicks off with Monroe's mandolin and then alternates intense solos from Scruggs's banjo and Chubby Wise's fiddle. It gave Scruggs the opportunity to show off the speed and accuracy that marked his banjo playing, with an opening passage on one take that sounded remarkably like "Foggy Mountain Breakdown."

Monroe's chattering mandolin and Wise's fluid fiddle complement Scruggs's banjo on the tune, Monroe's first instrumental recording with Scruggs on board. Flatt's guitar style, clearly audible on "Blue Grass Breakdown," was also key to the Blue Grass Boys sound. Banjo picker Jerry Keys, a longtime friend of Scruggs, pointed out to me, via a period photograph, that Flatt had used a flatpick on an archtop guitar in an earlier group, indicating a different approach from the bass-note and open-strings sound he employed with the Blue Grass Boys. According to Keys's account, Scruggs said that Monroe mandated the switch to thumb pick because he wanted Flatt to play like earlier Blue Grass Boys guitarist Clyde Moody. Moody's guitar work was featured on hits such as "Six White Horses."[5]

The music that the Blue Grass Boys produced in 1946 through 1948 stands with the most accomplished recorded pop music of the 20th century. It represents fulfilled destiny, as Monroe was able to achieve the drive, the bluesiness, the tempos and the feel—from breakdowns to gospel—that had been building in the modern processes of his mind. Like the poets and artists of the day, he was taking elements from a wide range of styles and creating a cohesive whole.

The sound would become known as bluegrass, although not until years later. Flatt and Scruggs took active parts in the development and broadened its scope, both while playing with Monroe and as their own act. Although the music of this incarnation of the Blue Grass Boys is considered traditional in the 21st century, when it was being created it was so revolutionary that it "sounded like a computer," as Ricky Skaggs once told me.

The live recordings that have circulated of the Blue Grass Boys during the Flatt and Scruggs tenure show the loud appreciation that Scruggs's three-finger banjo work won on the Opry. In the close confines of the Ryman Auditorium, the savvy audience seemed to have an almost physical reaction to the driving music, and members whooped and yelled at Scruggs's solos. He also caught the ear of Opry founder and announcer George D. Hay, who had always encouraged the most traditional of sounds on the WSM show.

"You remember him, 'The Solemn Old Judge'?" Scruggs asked, employing Hay's stage name. "He liked my picking, which was unusual for him. He was such a fan of old style, old-time—'Keep it down to earth!' was his slogan, you know.

"But he liked my picking. I remember some of the introductions he had—'Here's Earl Scruggs with his fancy five-string banjo and brother Bill with 'Little Joe,' or whatever it was we were going to do.'"[6]

Scruggs felt deceived by Monroe over "Blue Grass Breakdown" but also had problems with the band's relentless schedule of shows and the bandleader's unreliability. Monroe earned a public reputation as an upright symbol of professionalism in later years, but it was different in the early years, Scruggs said. As a young man used to hard work, Scruggs was in no mood to deal with slack behavior on the part of the fellow who was supposed to be the bossman.

"Oh, we missed a bunch of shows, sure did," Scruggs said.[7]

When the Blue Grass Boys finished their Saturday night Opry shows, they knew they'd be headed back on the road, but not exactly when.

"Standing around Saturday night, we'd want to know when we were gonna leave. Bill said, 'We'll leave midnight, tomorrow [Sunday] night.' Monroe liked to stay around the hotel until 5 p.m. Sundays, long after the band had checked out. Sometimes, the road trip wouldn't start until early Monday.

"I had to eat a real late supper and just sit in the lobby," Scruggs said. "I wasn't going to pay another two dollars a night for a room and not going to go to bed. And sometime I'd be sitting there when the sun came up the next morning, still waiting. He would not leave on time."

On one occasion that Scruggs recalled, Monroe couldn't get motivated to leave Hamilton, West Virginia, in time to appear on time for a date at a movie theater in Spartanburg, South Carolina.

"Goddang, I went in there, I never seen anybody more riled up than that manager was," Scruggs recalled of the band's arrival in Spartanburg.

"I said, 'I'm with Bill Monroe, where do we unload?'

"And he said, 'Is Bill Monroe here?'

"I said, 'Yes, sir, he's out there in the car.'

"'Does he know where he's playing tomorrow?'

"I said, 'Yes, sir, Charleston, South Carolina.'

"'You go tell him, if he'll start now he'll make Charleston. He ain't playing here.'"

Overall, Scruggs said, "You never saw anybody less professional than he was."

By 1947, his situation with Monroe had evidently grown so charged that Scruggs reached out to Mac Wiseman, then working at the powerful Bristol, Virginia, radio station WCYB.

"I came in to do the show one day, and this fellow came up to me," Wiseman said. "It was Earl Scruggs and he said that he and Chubby Wise were leaving Bill Monroe, and would I hire them?"[8]

Wiseman declined Scruggs's offer to join his band. But the incident shows that Scruggs's intention to leave Monroe had a significant gestation period, and that it didn't necessarily always involve Flatt. Wiseman would reappear before long in the Flatt and Scruggs saga.

A final incident that bothered Scruggs came even after he had given his notice, a professional arrangement that Monroe apparently entered on Scruggs's behalf without telling him.[9] Monroe asked him to remain for two extra weeks, and Scruggs agreed, not knowing that the bandleader had booked them both as named attractions on the nationally broadcast NBC Prince Albert Tobacco segment. Known as the "Prince Albert Show," this regular segment gave the Opry the nation's largest audience for country music.[10]

The Opry broadcast was so hot that the network had a waiting list of sponsors who wanted to buy time, but Prince Albert was among those who had been involved the longest. What Scruggs thought would be his last gig as a Blue Grass Boy turned out to be a spotlight that recognized his national reputation.

"Let's say Bill Monroe and the whole band would be there, and then they had me on for a tune," Scruggs said. "Bill did the first tune that started the show and I had the second tune. And I played 'Cumberland Gap.' I hadn't written anything at the time." Any extra money likely went to Monroe.

As host of the Prince Albert show, country star Red Foley said in introduction, "Our guests tonight, Bill Monroe and Earl Scruggs."

"They didn't bill Lester and Chubby and them," Scruggs said. "It was just whoever was doing these tunes got mentioned."

———

About the time of the Prince Albert episode, Flatt turned in his notice too, Scruggs said.

"He said, 'Well, I'm quitting too, Bill.'"

"And Monroe said, 'Well, I was going to give you a raise.'"

"Lester said, 'I could've used that, and Earl could, too. But I ain't staying for no raise. I'm leaving too.'"

In another little-known episode, Scruggs put in a brief stint with Opry star Roy Acuff before he left town, turning down Acuff's job offer as he left.[11]

Monroe was plainly disappointed at the loss of his talented side musicians. Curly Seckler recalled hearing the story from Flatt and Scruggs of Monroe's less-than-flattering attempts to keep Scruggs on.

"Bill even told Earl when he left that he'd never be worth nothing no more," Seckler said.

"'You're just my banjo picker and you'd better stay with me,'" Monroe told Scruggs.[12]

These longtime arguments and frustrations may seem far from central to the story of Scruggs and "Foggy Mountain Breakdown." However, Scruggs's discontent built to the point where he not only left a high-profile job with Monroe but also felt moved to create music that matched or surpassed that of his employer.

For his part, Monroe kept chasing great music. He remained tough competition for his wayward sons in bluegrass. By roughly 1950, he had hired such talented band members as singer-guitarists Wiseman and Jimmy Martin, fiddler Vassar Clements and Red Taylor, and banjo players Rudy Lyle and Don Reno.

Hard-core recordings such as "White House Blues," "The Little Girl and the Dreadful Snake," and "Memories of Mother and Dad," plus a series of inventive instrumentals, have convinced some fans that Monroe's best music followed that of the "classic" band. In addition, Monroe continued to experiment with chords, sounds, colorings, and other elements of his music for decades.

Scruggs always said that he and Flatt decided separately to leave Monroe's band, fed up with endless touring, low pay, and an unpredictable boss.

It was February 1948 when the soon-to-be partners left Monroe and Nashville heading east, with Scruggs envisioning a return to a textile-mill job that was easier than the life he'd been living. The Monroe years had left them bone-weary; travel was so constant that, as Scruggs often said, they'd go for long spells without taking off their shoes. When they did get rooms, they didn't have the luxury of singles.

"We roomed together all the time, and back then we couldn't afford a room apiece," Scruggs said. "And me and Lester would get a room for, I'd say, three dollars. That was two dollars for a single and three dollars for a double.

"So we'd split that, a dollar and a half apiece and both sleep in the same bed. Oh yeah, we stayed together all the time."

Along with the freedom they felt in leaving Monroe, the friends must have had some trepidation about quitting steady work.

"Bill, you know, was just paying what sounded like a lot of money . . . sixty dollars a week," Scruggs said. "But I was having hotel bills seven nights a week and eating out of restaurants. And back then you didn't have stay-press clothes, and dry-cleaning was extremely high. Having your pants pressed, and you wouldn't sit down 'til after the show because once you did that the imprint would still be in your pants."

Flatt and Scruggs had been part of a band that built the foundation of bluegrass. But that Monroe quintet never again played together. Their sound came to an end when Flatt and Scruggs departed.

Many years later, Monroe would dismiss their contributions as cofounders of the music. In 1989 he talked backstage at the Grand Ole Opry, where he had just completed a *Rolling Stones* photo shoot with Chris Hillman, famous as a founder of the Byrds rock band. Hillman was also a decades-long bluegrass fan and picker, as well as a current country star as a member of the Desert Rose Band. He and Monroe were photographed together for a magazine spread on stars and their mentors.

"What was that feller's name?" Monroe asked after Hillman left.

It was one of many situations in which it wasn't clear whether Monroe was sincere or joking. But he seemed entirely serious on the same occasion when asked about the contribution Lester Flatt and Earl Scruggs had made to bluegrass.

"Bluegrass was already going when they got in the picture," Monroe said. "They didn't have a thing to do with bluegrass music, getting it going the way it's going. The fast time of the music and everything was there."

So, Flatt and Scruggs were just two more players in the long roster of Blue Grass Boys? "They had a job," Monroe said with a nod.

And what about "Blue Grass Breakdown"?

"'Blue Grass Breakdown,' that's a fine number," Monroe said. "Then Earl wrote a number called 'Foggy Mountain Breakdown' and he played the same part as I did until he came down off and I went in F and he went in E minor."

The "coming down off" that Monroe referred to was the change from the G major chord at the heart of both tunes to either the Em or F chord, both lower chords considering the note played on the low E string of the guitar.

"That wasn't no trouble for him to write that, because it was already ahead of him, part of it," Monroe said of 'Foggy Mountain Breakdown.'"

Coupled with what Scruggs said in 2007, the two greatest pickers of bluegrass each maintained that the other had in effect appropriated his rival's classic tune. In any case, Scruggs wound up with his name on the higher-profile number, "Foggy Mountain Breakdown."

7

FLATT AND SCRUGGS
BUILD A CAREER

It had been a gamble for Flatt and Scruggs to stow their instruments in worn cases and leave Nashville and Bill Monroe. He had kept them busy, whatever else he may have done. In heading back east, they lost the powerful Grand Ole Opry brand. Years would pass before they regained it.

Scruggs said later that at 24 he had wanted to be more helpful and closer to his mother, Lula, and half-sister, Venie Mae, whom he'd been helping support with his Blue Grass Boy wages. He even worked toward buying a house and a couple of lots for them in Shelby.[1] However, some form of collaboration seems to have been building in the friends' minds. It wasn't long before Flatt called and suggested that they head out on their own. Flatt and Scruggs were an atypical duo—a lead singer and an instrumentalist/ background singer—whose discipline and talent brought success beyond any expectations.

The band got started in the show-business hinterlands of Hickory, North Carolina; Danville, Virginia; and Bristol, Tennessee. Playing radio stations at dawn and schoolhouses or movie theaters at noon or night, they kicked their level of musicianship upward to draw audiences and eventually to sell records. The music updated the Southern string-band sound based on the creativity of Flatt's songwriting and Scruggs's instrumental skills.

By way of contrast, traditional New Orleans jazz, another regional music that possessed great power and creativity, lost much of its original spark as elements of it became known as Dixieland, a more commercial, often cornball sound.

"I think one of the main reasons that bluegrass didn't get hokey is because of that black influence that Bill Monroe had and that Earl had, whether he knew it or not," modern banjo stylist Béla Fleck said. "The influence was embedded in the music. Earl, he had a natural funk in his playing. There was something very old in what he did."[2]

Fleck and others have traced the banjo's origins to Africa, hearing elements of the akonting's drone string and bluesy slides in the styles that had been adopted in Appalachia. Scruggs's rapid tempos on the instrument gave those centuries-old elements and percussive rhythms an infusion of 20th century drive. His style also injected bent notes and outside-the-bar-line rhythmic jumps into more conventional compositions. His three-finger roll kept everything in smooth motion.

During their 21 years as musical partners, Flatt and Scruggs would surpass their former boss and every other bluegrass-style act in popularity. "There was two giants in that, Lester and Earl," longtime band member Curly Seckler said. "I give them both credit. They created what they did. Nobody was doing that, Bill [Monroe] wasn't doing what they were doing."[3]

The name for their band was drawn from the Carter Family song "Foggy Mountain Top." Recorded by the Monroe Brothers in 1936, the song is attributed to A. P. Carter but likely descends from the English tune, "The Rocky Mountain Top."[4] That means that the song, and subsequently the band name and the reference in "Foggy Mountain Breakdown," likely do not spring from any specific American locale, as fulfilling as it might be to visit the scene of the breakdown. Carmen, North Carolina, where Cecil Sharp collected "Rocky Mountain Top," is north of Asheville, nearly in Tennessee.

The Foggy Mountain Boys debuted in Danville, Scruggs recalled. The accomplished bassist and comedian Howard Watts had also left Monroe and joined Flatt and Scruggs. The country-tinged singer-guitarist Jim Eanes made it a quartet. "There were just the four of us and we were only there two or three weeks," Scruggs told historian Barry R. Willis. "We called Jim Shumate, wanting a fiddle player. He wanted us to come to Hickory to work on a radio station there. He was working in a furniture store in Hickory and didn't want to leave. We were there just a matter of weeks."[5]

Wiseman called Scruggs looking for a job and joined them in Hickory, a location that was attractive to Scruggs because it was only a short drive away from his family in Shelby.

But Wiseman, who kept in touch with the market, persuaded them to take a chance by moving the band to radio station WCYB in Bristol, where he had built a track record. Founded in 1946, the station became a prime breeding ground for acts in the spring-green bluegrass style. Flatt and Scruggs arrived in Bristol, right on the Tennessee-Virginia line, about the last of April or the first of May 1948, Scruggs said. "That was a hot station," Scruggs said, "We had a hot band then. Started making money right off the reel."

=====

The period in Bristol was remarkable for several reasons. Flatt and Scruggs were stepping into the middle of a competitive scene. Only a few bands were playing bluegrass music and they often behaved like rivals. Interviewed in 2016, Jesse McReynolds remembered that the Stanley Brothers, then the headline act at WCYB, had a rule against their band members' so much as talking to pickers in other groups.

"Back then there wasn't that much communication between country and bluegrass bands," McReynolds said, adding, "We always tried to get along with everybody."[6]

Jesse and brother Jim McReynolds, who became an enduring hit act as Jim & Jesse, didn't pass the WCYB audition and were playing at a lower-powered competitor. But even the well-established Stanleys had reason to worry when an act as experienced and driven as Flatt and Scruggs came to town.

Jesse McReynolds recalled sitting in a restaurant across the street from WCYB's studio while Flatt and Scruggs played their audition. Pee Wee Lambert, the mandolinist and singer for the Stanleys, came over and spoke to Jim and Jesse, despite the ban.

"Reckon they'll get on?" Lambert asked, referring to the chance that Flatt and Scruggs would earn a spot on the station.

"We said, 'Yeah, reckon they will,'" Jesse McReynolds said wryly.

=====

Along with growing audiences and gigs came a semblance of financial stability for Flatt and Scruggs. And for Scruggs, those days in Bristol brought marriage. According to his often-told tale, he had spotted young Louise Certain while on stage working with Bill Monroe at the Opry in 1946. They married on April 18, 1948, while the band was at WCYB.

"We got us an apartment there in Bristol, and the first year about the only thing we had to move when we moved was a suitcase apiece," Scruggs said. "Then the suitcases start getting too small. After a while you have to get two suitcases."

Louise Scruggs was to play a vital role in Earl's personal and professional life for nearly 60 years. Louise and Earl were suited to each other in intelligence, energy, and the desire to center their lives on a strong family. By 1949, Louise would give birth to their first child, son Gary. And, vitally, she eventually took over Earl's role of booking jobs, at which she was to gain formidable expertise.

In March 1949, the *Kingsport News* reported the sale of nine surplus trailers that had been used to house military veterans after the war. The average price of the trailers was $130, but Earl Scruggs paid the most for one, at $252, a rare instance of his paying more than necessary for anything.[7] Jerry Keys related the story as he heard it from Scruggs: The auctioneer had mentioned that the trailers went for about $250 in a sealed-bid process, so the usually cautious Earl threw in an extra $2 to make sure he got the new home for his family.[8]

The period must have meant a whirlwind of an existence for Scruggs: starting a family, playing WCYB and many resulting gigs, putting out songbooks, and booking shows. He also kept a close ear to the sound and musicianship in the band.

Flatt and Scruggs were crafting a distinctive style, deliberately separating themselves from Monroe as time passed. Another aspect of the split with Monroe was clear to Scruggs, he said emphatically more than half a lifetime later: There was more satisfaction and enjoyment for Flatt and Scruggs in running their own show than in working in Monroe's shadow.

The late 1940s also saw the arrival of two new Foggy Mountain Boys. Former Monroe side musician Art Wooten came to the band on fiddle. On mandolin and vocals came Seckler, a man who would work for decades with many of the best bluegrass players. From China Grove, North Carolina, Seckler had a smashing tenor voice and capable mandolin and guitar skills as well as a notable sense of humor.

Seckler's story about how he got hired shows how small the circles were, and how heated the competition, among those early high-powered string bands. The tale started at WCYB.

"They was working there when I was working with Charlie Monroe," Seckler said. "[Flatt and Scruggs] had a program on there; they'd come out and Charlie and us we would go in, and we wasn't allowed to speak to 'em. Ain't that something? We wasn't allowed to speak to them."

Who laid down the law about the contact?

"Oh, Charlie didn't want you speaking to them," Seckler said. "Lester finally got around to where we would talk a little bit, and Lester asked me, 'I'd like to have you to sing with me. You've got a voice out of this world.' He said, 'Mac [Wiseman] is going to go.' But he didn't say how quick."[9]

Meanwhile, Seckler left Charlie Monroe for a job with Jim and Jesse McReynolds, who had started a band in Augusta, Georgia. That outfit included Scruggs's former employer Wiley Morris and the influential banjoist Hoke Jenkins, the cousin of Snuffy Jenkins.

In a glimpse into the economic realities of the bluegrass business in the late 1940s, Wiseman said in 2015 that he exited the Foggy Mountain Boys after Flatt and Scruggs said they wanted to put him and the other musicians on a weekly salary, instead of splitting the proceeds equally as before.

"I said, 'Hell, no—I ain't going to work for you sons of bitches on salary,'" Wiseman said, laughing at the memory. "I went down to WSB in Atlanta and I had daily radio shows of my own."[10]

Needing a strong singer to replace Wiseman, Flatt soon called Seckler.

"Lester called me about going up there," Seckler said. "He said, 'How soon can you get up here?'"[11]

"I said, 'We've got to make a deal first.'

"He said, 'There won't be no problem on that.'" Accepting Flatt's assurance, Seckler rode a bus from Georgia to Bristol and became a Foggy Mountain Boy in March 1949.

That same month, Bill Monroe and the Blue Grass Boys released a new 78 rpm disc: the rocketing "Toy Heart," with none other than "Blue Grass

Breakdown" on the other side. That meant Flatt and Scruggs would have heard their own playing featured on the 1947 Monroe instrumental. That it was a tune Scruggs considered his own, and a copyright that was earning royalties for Monroe, would not have been lost on the business-minded pair.

Monroe maintained a relationship of sorts with his former bandmates, only firmly turning his back on them when they landed on his home turf of the Grand Ole Opry in 1955.[12]

In fact, Monroe's visit to a Flatt and Scruggs radio show at WCYB in Bristol led to what's known as the Swap, the best-known exchange of instruments in bluegrass history.

Jim Mills related the story as he had assembled it from various sources.[13] "Flatt and Scruggs were a newly formed band. They had left Monroe, they were playing WCYB, and Don Reno was playing banjo for Bill Monroe," Mills said. "Bill is coming through the area. They invite him on their show to plug a few of his dates.

"Earl had been after that banjo for years. Don always said Earl never had a banjo that was up to snuff enough for him to make the trade. Meanwhile, when Earl was playing with Bill Monroe, he acquired a Gibson RB-75. It was like brand new almost.

"And when Don Reno saw this banjo and Earl inquired about trading banjos again, there at Bristol's radio station, the Granada was in poor condition, the plating was bad, and the tension hoop was cracked. It had a lot of problems, a lot of wear on it. It had been owned by Fisher Hendley, Snuffy Jenkins, and then Don had had it for several years. But Earl heard something special in that banjo.

"He wanted it, even though he had an almost brand-new condition, shiny new RB-75 [Gibson banjo]. Don said, 'Sure I'll trade with you. I'll even throw a guitar in because this banjo's in kind of rough shape.'"

Apparently the trade took place in 1949, just months before the December recording of "Foggy Mountain Breakdown." The banjo acquired in the swap, once repaired and set up to Scruggs's satisfaction, became his principal instrument for the rest of his career.

———

After a series of moves, Flatt and Scruggs joined the "Kentucky Mountain Barn Dance" radio show in Lexington in November 1949, playing broadcasts each Saturday night.[14]

They were recording for Mercury, a new label. Mercury's "artists and repertoire" man Murray Nash had been using a facility called Herzog Recording Studios, not far from Lexington in downtown Cincinnati.

Everything was coming together. Scruggs had the technique, the drive, the band and the banjo. His new "Foggy Mountain Breakdown" was a fast-paced tune using the G to E minor chord sequence on his powerful Granada. Flatt and Scruggs were playing the tune on stage, and it appeared on the list of songs they were to record at Herzog, on a Sunday that likely followed a Saturday night gig in Lexington. Cincinnati and the recording session lay about 80 miles north, perhaps a two-hour drive under the conditions of the day. The trip that would produce a recording that lives in American music history.

8

RECORDING "FOGGY MOUNTAIN BREAKDOWN"

With a strong band and fresh musical approach, Flatt and Scruggs needed to make records of their own to reach the level of recognition and success they had enjoyed with Monroe on the Grand Ole Opry. They had played on great records as Blue Grass Boys, but not yet with their Foggy Mountain Boys.

They were to sign with Mercury Records, but not before another label tried to sign them.

Music business man Syd Nathan, head of the freewheeling King Records label in Cincinnati and an eventual member of the Rock and Roll Hall of Fame, approached the Foggy Mountain crew about re-creating the sound of Bill Monroe and the Blue Grass Boys. He had already induced other acts to remake popular recordings for his label. "King offered us a deal and wanted us to do the [Bill] Monroe stuff," Mac Wiseman recalled. "He had Hawkshaw Hawkins doing [Ernest] Tubb. In 1947, he wanted me to do Monroe material. I knew I'd never get anywhere as a copy."[1] Flatt, however, was in favor of accepting King's 1948 offer for Flatt and Scruggs to reprise their former sound with Monroe, Wiseman recalled: "He wanted to show Monroe he could get going fast." The deal with King never materialized.

In autumn 1948, when Flatt and Scruggs were approached by Mercury, the music business was entering a hustling phase, marked by postwar energy, technical savvy, and interest in new developments in several styles of music. The American Federation of Musicians recording bans of 1942–1944 and 1948 had been resolved, and players were again allowed to take part in recording sessions under union contracts.[2]

The accomplished Flatt and Scruggs team sounded like a hot property, at least to the ears of record man Nash, 30 years old and a go-getter from his early days in the Midwest and Tennessee.[3] Well-dressed men like Nash signed promising artists, recorded them in several different cities, and traveled the landscape taking promotional 78 rpm discs to radio stations, department stores, and music emporiums. Record promoters put in thousands of miles to push records to prosperous postwar audiences. Nash had entered the music business as sales manager for retail records for the successful Knoxville hardware store McClung's. He quickly became familiar with Nashville, the Grand Ole Opry, showbiz media, and the music business. By 1947, he was director of folk music, the current industry term for country, for the startup Mercury, immersing himself in the hard work and addictive energy of the music business.

☰

Mercury had been started in Chicago by Irving Green, who had been born into the business as son of New York–based National Records owner Al Green, whom Nash described as "probably a questionable character."[4] Irving Green was an innovator who started a record-pressing plant in the Windy City using the boiler of a next-door dry cleaner to power the manufacturing process. Nash's account of Mercury's promotional efforts, at least in Chicago, seemed to reflect the gangster connections that have long shadowed the music business. The business approach appeared at first to be a sort of low-level villainy, far from the murderous bandits to be linked to bluegrass by "Foggy Mountain Breakdown." But according to Nash, the ties to gangland were real enough.

"A fellow by the name of Sneeze Friedman, who was an ex–Al Capone man, one of the very few that ever got out of the ring, was their salesman, and he would load these 78s that Irv had pressed the night before in the back of an old Oldsmobile convertible and head around to the record shops," Nash said. "If it was a small shop, he just took one box of 25 records and walked in, put them on the counter, and told the clerk this was their order from Mercury Records. The clerk wondered who Mercury Records was. They hadn't ordered anything from Mercury. Well, with his hand in his coat pocket and lifted slightly, Chicago style, he said, 'This is your order from Mercury Records, and that will be $19.' 'Oh, yeah, sure,' the clerk said, so the $19 was paid off."

Nash recalled the day Friedman double-parked in front of the Mercury office, blocking a streetcar, then told an enquiring police office that the passengers could wait: Sneeze was operating "with connections." Sneeze Friedman sounds like a character straight out of a B movie, too bad to be true. However, the *Chicago Daily Tribune* reported in May 1948 that Leo "Sneeze" Friedman had been shot to death in what was described as a gangland retribution slaying unconnected to the label. Mercury co-chief Arthur Talmadge denied to the *Tribune* a report that Friedman worked for the company.[5]

Despite, or perhaps because of, its backroom connections, Mercury's pop division started thriving with pop recordings by the likes of Frankie Laine, a former singing waiter who hit it big with "Mule Train." And Patti Page, the sweetly intimate chanteuse, scored a hit for the ages with "Tennessee Waltz." But hillbilly music? "They didn't understand it," Nash said of Mercury's Chicago-based leadership. "They couldn't understand doing a session down there in Cincinnati without pre-planning and written arrangements and getting a producer to go in there and wave his hand while they're playing and so on."[6]

═══

Though an upstart label, Mercury employed such talented record men as a young Mitch Miller, who was to make sing-along a national craze, and, briefly, the legendary John Hammond, discoverer of artists from Billie Holiday to Stevie Ray Vaughn. Mercury took a freewheeling approach to the music with divisions for pop, classical, country, and "race," or rhythm and blues. Unlike executives at established labels such as RCA Victor, Mercury executives and producers seemed little inclined to hover over their country acts, to make them record any specific kinds of material, or to guide their style. Nash was allowed to record what he thought would sell, and he trusted Flatt and Scruggs to come into the studio with their best material. There's a parallel here with the early days of rock, with British invasion acts and the elliptical Bob Dylan and psychedelic acts such as Jefferson Airplane and the Grateful Dead: The music grew strongest when labels knew too little about it to take creative control.

Nash had experience with a number of different musical approaches, working with artists including Pee Wee King of "Tennessee Waltz" fame and Scruggs's fellow Cleveland County native Don Gibson, a brilliant songwriter and singer. Nash was also to work with jazz and blues musicians including New Orleans' Roy Byrd, later known as Professor Longhair. Based in Knoxville, Nash paid attention to the local scene but had his ear caught by a broadcasting band: Lester Flatt and Earl Scruggs and the Foggy Mountain Boys. "I heard them on the radio, WBIR in Knoxville," Nash told Country Music Foundation historian John Rumble. "They had an early morning show, and I heard them on the radio and went and talked to them."

Rumble asked: "Just called on them and said, 'How would you like to record for Mercury?'" As simple as that, Nash said: "Yeah, told them I wanted them as an artist, wanted to record them on Mercury. At that time, they hadn't thought about recording at all. They were busy with their personal appearances, which were mostly schoolhouses within a 50- or 60-mile radius of Knoxville, their early morning radio show, and that kept them busy. They hadn't worried about recording, and it more or less surprised them for somebody to walk up and want to make records with them."

Here it seems that Nash's recollection might not have been entirely spot on. Flatt and Scruggs had appeared on several strong-selling discs with Monroe and were well aware of the exposure and royalties that could result from a record deal. In the same interview, Nash said he signed Flatt and Scruggs to a one-year contract with two additional yearly options. In effect it was a three-year contract that wound up lasting a little more than two.

Flatt, Scruggs, and the Foggy Mountain Boys cut their first Mercury session in fall 1948, at radio station WROL in Knoxville, where they were making regular appearances.[7] The session took place in what is now the imposing Holston apartment building at 531 Gay Street, across the street from the East Tennessee Historical Society. (City directories in the museum list Flatt's and Scruggs's residences on rural Rutledge Pike during the same years.)

With Wiseman on board, as well as Shumate and Watts, they cut four memorable tunes: "We'll Meet Again Sweetheart," "Cabin in Caroline," "God

Loves His Children" and "I'm Going to Make Heaven My Home." Just as Monroe had taken a while to arrive at a specific sound, Flatt and Scruggs were experimenting with different approaches. For example, Scruggs played fingerpicking guitar instead of five-string banjo on two of those first Mercury tracks. Scruggs's fine guitar playing is worth much more discussion, but it should at least be noted that his style combines a lot of Maybelle Carter, a good bit of Merle Travis, and portions of his own banjo style. The crisp guitar heard on "God Loves His Children" and "I'm Going to Make Heaven My Home" would form a central element of the Flatt and Scruggs sound. "We'll Meet Again Sweetheart," a strong Flatt and Wiseman duet," and "Cabin in Caroline" became bluegrass standards. Scruggs and the instrumental crew displayed a smooth, yet powerful ensemble sound.

By spring 1949, the Foggy Mountain Boys were in a new city, Cincinnati, to record four more enduring tunes: "Baby Blue Eyes," "Bouquet in Heaven," "Down the Road" and "Why Don't You Tell Me So." "Down the Road" has significance because of its use of an E minor or relative minor chord. It was among the first such uses, if not the first, by the first-generation bluegrass bands. Their next use of the chord came with "Foggy Mountain Breakdown."

Today, Cincinnati offers several reminders of itself in 1949—a city of industry, a soup of many cultures and a pop-music capital of sorts. The ornate building that housed the far-reaching radio station WLW still looms over the corner of Ninth and Elm streets, and many popular-music auditoriums of that day are still standing, if not active. Brian Powers, a music historian who works with the Cincinnati Public Library, gave me a tour of the area on a bitterly cold day, pointing out significant spots from downtown to Over-the-Rhine. That neighborhood, across the Miami Canal from downtown, has been on the rebound. Its name refers to the Rhine river, a reminder of the many Germans who populated the neighborhood in the 19th century. That group of immigrants was gradually replaced by Appalachian transplants and other working-class families.[8] The hillbilly influx would give Cincinnati an enduring audience for country and bluegrass music.

Chief among the colorful cast of 1940s Cincinnati music figures was Syd Nathan, the freewheeling industry pioneer who started King Records in 1943 and tried to sign Flatt and Scruggs in 1948. Nathan made his name at King by recording everyone from the Delmore Brothers to Hank Ballard and the Midnighters, from the Stanley Brothers to James Brown. "By 1944, Syd has a record plant, but he doesn't have a studio," Powers said. "Syd was doing recordings in Los Angeles. He had Grandpa Jones out there in spring 1946." Meanwhile, E. T. "Bud" Herzog, an engineer at radio station Cincinnati WLW, had started a studio, at first in his home. As King Records was catching fire, Herzog was getting enough work from Nathan and others to move his second-job studio from his home to Race Street in downtown. The *Cincinnati Enquirer* announced the facility's opening on May 26, 1946.[9] Herzog engineered recordings for national labels Capital, Columbia and RCA Victor.

Herzog had an impressive list of clients. The studio's output included sides by Hank Williams, Patti Page, Rosemary Clooney, and others. Williams went to Cincinnati to make records even after he had started his recording career at Castle Studios, the name given to a "no-frills converted dining room"[10] at the old Tulane Hotel in downtown Nashville.[11]

≡≡≡

The second floor of the Race Street building still houses the control room and recording space of the former Herzog room, but they are no longer walled off. Operated in recent years as a sort of Cincinnati music museum, the second floor is open for occasional events. Framed posters and photos of the river town's music scene line the walls. Elliot Ruther of the Cincinnati USA Music Heritage Foundation provided a tour, mentioning that the rent is paid by a donor who doesn't want to be identified. The E. W. Herzog Recording Studio was the spot where Murray Nash, very likely, plugged his two-piece magnetic tape recorder into the studio's board, taking out a monaural feed that combined signals from as many as four microphones plugged into the board. The recording took place during changing times for technology and for music industry practices, both of which benefited Flatt and Scruggs.

During one of several Country Music Foundation interviews he gave in the 1970s and '80s, Nash provided specifics about his recording setup. Researcher John Rumble asked how many microphones Nash used to record Flatt and Scruggs. "In their case, I think we set up four and used three," Nash said. "Of course, we had to have one for fiddle. We had to have one for the banjo. We had to have vocal. Lester and Earl would play close together, so we'd get enough of Lester's guitar in the banjo mic. Then one for the bass, and that was about what we had."[12]

Magnetic tape recording was in its first year or so of wide commercial availability in the United States in 1949. Pop culture star Bing Crosby had researched it and was promoting the technology. Finding that tape recording, principally developed by German scientists over several decades, worked better and offered more flexibility than transcription disks, Crosby helped start the Ampex company and by 1948 was using its products to record his network broadcasts. The Magnecord machine that Nash used to record "Foggy Mountain Breakdown" had just been introduced the previous year.[13]

Various accounts of the "Foggy Mountain Breakdown" recording session have placed it at King Studios or at an unnamed radio station, but there's no hard evidence to back those claims. Based on an interview with Herzog himself, John Hartley Fox's book, *King of the Queen City*, locates the session at Herzog Recording.[14] For most followers of Flatt and Scruggs, of bluegrass, and of sound recording, Nash's approach as described differs from accepted wisdom about single-mic approaches to recording and performing. A couple of generations of bluegrass bands, starting in the 1980s, made a practice of performing grouped around one microphone. Wheeling in and out and among each other, they professed that the single large-condenser mic approach amounted to performing "just like Lester and Earl did it." Except Lester and Earl didn't, at least in the studio, according to Nash's account.

Controversy remains about the evolution in recording techniques, as Nash was vague in his interviews about exactly when the multiple-mic recording approach was used. To sum up, he said he used the Magnecord tape recorder in the 1948 Knoxville sessions, before the Herzog recordings. After the "Foggy Mountain Breakdown" recording, he used that machine with three to four mics in Tampa, Florida, for the 1950 "hurricane" sessions that were his last with Flatt and Scruggs. It seems logical that the session between, at Herzog, would have employed the same approach.

"We got this Magnecorder, the first tape machine, in Chicago, and I carried that around with me. I would record anywhere from basements to radio stations, setting my equipment up and running through their mixer, their panel," Nash said. There's no mention in the Country Music Foundation interviews of the setup in Cincinnati. But given the clear, balanced sound of "Foggy Mountain Breakdown" and the other December 11, 1949, recordings, those tracks likely represent the multimicrophone-to-tape approach in one of its earliest incarnations. Flatt and Scruggs's woven ensemble sound might have been designed to make good use of this new technique.

The Foggy Mountain Boys were booked into Herzog for two sessions on that Sunday.

The band had been working steadily, playing every Saturday night—except Christmas Eve—between November 5, 1949, and January 21, 1950, at the Kentucky Mountain Barn Dance in Lexington.[15] The band was also broadcasting over WVLK in Versailles, Kentucky, and playing every available gig. When the Clay-Gentry Stockyards, their sponsors on the Kentucky Mountain Barn Dance, stopped broadcasting the show, Flatt and Scruggs started a similar show on another station, until Clay-Gentry won a court injunction to stop them. Here was evidence that the band's popularity was a commodity worth suing over.[16]

When the Foggy Mountain Boys hit the Herzog studio, they were ready and their sound was crackling. "They were exceptionally easy to record," Nash said. "They had their arrangements down, the whole works. About the only thing we had to do was run through it and get it for time. In other words, if it ran too long, we'd cut something out. If it wasn't long enough, we'd sing the bridge twice." In 2002, Scruggs told *Cincinnati Enquirer* reporter Larry Nager that "Foggy Mountain Breakdown" was his favorite of the many recordings he'd made. But more crucially for banjo pickers and hard-core fans of the tune, Scruggs also recalled some details of that December day, including the "lousy weather." The *Enquirer* predicted a bad day for banjos in that day's edition: "Occasional rain and warmer," with temperatures between 48 and 60 degrees Fahrenheit.

"Back in those days, the banjos had skin heads on 'em, those calfskin heads," Scruggs told Nager. "And when it was a clear day, the banjo could really strut its stuff. But let it turn like low pressure, get damp and foggy, rainy, that head would get soggy on you and that tone would start leaving. What I did was put a light bulb in the back of the banjo and dried it out. It brought that good, snappy tone to it."

Curly Seckler also remembered Scruggs's practice of holding the banjo to a light bulb to get its tension up to muster. At shows, Scruggs sometimes exposed the banjo to stage lights to achieve the same result.

"We used all my equipment, and I had a little $14 microphone that we always recorded the banjo on," Nash said. "It was a different banjo sound because of that heated head, and it was all done on this. That was Earl's special microphone. It cost $14, and that was what those early Flatt and Scruggs things were done on." Bert van Oortmarssen, from the Netherlands, an expert on vintage microphones, said that Shure, Astatic, Turner, and other makers produced models in the $14 price range in the late '40s that could have done the job. If Scruggs had been using a less taut banjo head on the session, there's a chance we might not be talking about the performance today. Banjoist Tom McKinney has said the Mastertone on "Foggy Mountain Breakdown" sounds like "firecrackers going off in a Number 10 washtub."

Lester Flatt's Martin D-28, which rolls along in step with Watts's pumping bass and the strong chop of Seckler's mandolin, probably sported at least a fresh G string. Scruggs recalled that Flatt hit his familiar "G-run" so often that he replaced that string more often than any other. Details of the "Foggy Mountain Breakdown" session, just one of many dozens for Flatt and Scruggs and the band at the time, eluded Scruggs and Seckler when I interviewed them decades later. But the recording they made remains explosive to this day. The 78 rpm release, Mercury 6247, summons a lot of notes and overtones out of the speakers of a good system. Hearing the original 78 on period or compatible equipment is an experience that listeners should seek out if possible. Every instrument remains present and nuanced.

Nash apparently had the ability to "ride," or change the volume of, the individual channels as the recording progressed. The signals couldn't be mixed after the recording, so the technology was still many miles from the fingertip control of every musical element that producers had by the late 1960s. But the approach of recording several mics to tape and Nash's work on the mic signals, coupled with a great performance, produced music that has stood up to critical assessment for many decades. Country Music Foundation interviewer Doug Green, also known as Ranger Doug of the cowboy band Riders in the Sky, remarked to Nash in 1983 that countless other studios and acts had strived to re-create the full-throated twang of the Flatt and Scruggs Mercury sides. Nash said: "I think it was generally felt in the business, at least it was told to me several times, that the old Mercury things were the best Flatt and Scruggs things that were recorded."[17]

That December session resulted in a March 1950 78 rpm release of "Foggy Mountain Breakdown" that earned a one-sentence review in the show business bible *Billboard*. The reviewer, according to Nash's account of the *Billboard* staffing of the day, was quite likely a young, music-hungry figure named Jerry Wexler. Within three years, Wexler would join the nascent Atlantic label as a producer, cutting countless hits for everyone from the Drifters to Dire Straits. Rock and Roll Hall of Fame member Wexler is not often associated with country music. But in June 1949, he displayed broad musical taste and had been in on changing the name of the *Billboard* "hillbilly" chart to "country & western," just as he helped change the black-oriented music known as "race" to "rhythm & blues."

The *Billboard* take on "Foggy Mountain Breakdown"? "Getoff banjo is spotlighted in a fast moving country stomper," the entire review read.[18] "Getoff" presumably was used to denote a hot or improvised instrumental performance, a feature also referred to as a "takeoff" passage at the time. According to Scruggs, his three-finger banjo approach had come to him, as if in a dream, at his old Flint Hill home back in Carolina, some 15 years earlier. "Foggy Mountain Breakdown," perhaps the best-known example of that style, was available starting in 1950 to anyone who hit the right record store with three or four quarters in hand. And the impact of "Foggy Mountain Breakdown" would expand in quantum jumps, amid strokes of fortune and decades of cultural change.

9

"LIKE A JACKHAMMER"—
HOW THE TUNE WORKS

It begins with just a "pinch," the percussive effect created when a banjo player hits a down stroke with the thumb pick along with an upstroke with at least one finger pick, so the strings ring as one. There was no "One-two-three" count-off to guide them, so the four other musicians seemed to scramble to catch up after Earl Scruggs, at 25, kicked off his new banjo instrumental "Foggy Mountain Breakdown." As for the abrupt beginning, key sideman Curly Seckler knew what that signified. Scruggs kicked it off by himself, just as he would have on a show after a few words of introduction from Flatt. "Lester was as good an announcer as a man would ever want," Seckler told me. "He was great with his talking. He would just say so much and that was it. For instance, if he was talking a little bit, he'd say, 'We got Earl Scruggs here now; we're going to get him to pick the 'Foggy Mountain Breakdown.' Earl was done gone. Just that quick. There was no messing around."

From its rainy Sunday start, the tune caught on. Its popularity at first came gradually, and as the '50s, '60s and '70s proceeded, swelled to became part of the general musical consciousness of America and of places far beyond. The endurance of "Foggy Mountain Breakdown" as a piece of music rests on a number of interwoven factors. "A banjo tune was kind of a certain kind of melody—you need to let the banjo ring," said Tim O'Brien, singer-songwriter, picker, and longtime member of the band Hot Rize, as well as being an original member of the Flatt and Scruggs revival act, the Earls of Leicester. "If you have too many chords, it kind of stops it. When you hear 'Foggy Mountain Breakdown,' you're hearing an awful lot of really good banjo playing. With all the things that are in it, there's a lot of subtlety. [Scruggs] was so well ordered that everything he played is put forward in a greatly refined way. It just translates. It seems like he wasn't trying hard; it's like sleight of hand."[1]

Scruggs's technique indeed let his Granada ring and made the most of the rolling chords at the heart of "Foggy Mountain Breakdown." (The five-string banjo as used in bluegrass, beginning with the short fifth string, is tuned to G above middle C, then the "low" D below middle C, then G, B, and D, a whole step up from middle C.) The performance isn't all about power. There's generosity in the rounded distinction Scruggs lends to each note, no matter how rapidly it's hit.

He keeps a melody going amid the torrent of sixteenth notes, sometimes breaking the flow with eighth notes. Compared to "Blue Grass Breakdown," "Foggy Mountain Breakdown" has a much clearer strain; it's almost hummable. That element goes back to Scruggs's childhood, he said. He often recalled an exchange he had with his mother, Lula, herself a musician, as he played the same bluesy tune repeatedly at the family home one day.[2] The song was "Step It Up and Go," an energetic landmark tune by Blind Boy Fuller, the African American guitarist and singer from Durham. In general, blues-based soloing tends to lean more strongly on bent tones, rhythmic repetition, and textures than on melodies per se.

"I heard this first rock and roll tune, or it could be called that, I guess, 'Step It Up and Go.' I got to playing that thing, and, boy, to me I was hearing all the parts, but nobody was there with a guitar or anything, to put the other chords in.

"My mama said, 'Earl, if you're going to play something, play something that's got a tune to it.' And that was a good statement to make to me. And I got to thinking, 'God dang, if my own mother can't tell what I'm playing, I'm doing something wrong.'

"I don't always do it—but I want somebody to play the tune, you know. 'Cause if you lose the public, that's the ones that buys the groceries."

Music that's strongly conceived can be appreciated at a variety of levels. That's the case with "Foggy Mountain Breakdown." At its most basic it's a succession of right-hand rolls and licks played over three chords for 16 bars, 13 times, with a brief "tag" to round it out. But there's much more to it, as countless banjo pickers have learned from repeated hearings of Scruggs and the Foggy Mountain Boys at work.

On the recording, Flatt employed his typical guitar technique, an old-fashioned approach with a thumb pick and one fingerpick that few current bluegrass guitarists use. It contains elements of Maybelle Carter's technique. North Carolina–born Andy Griffith can be seen using a similar guitar style on some of the many reruns of his television show. At the end of certain bars, Flatt hit a distinctive bass run that ends in a ringing open G string. It's what came to be called "the Lester Flatt G run," and it chased the galloping banjo like a hound in full cry.

"His main thing was that G run," Scruggs told me in 2007, humming the bass-strings figure Flatt played. "He'd change third strings about every time we did a show, because that was his main string to hit."

In 2007 Scruggs criticized Flatt's guitar playing, but not on "Foggy Mountain Breakdown."

"One thing hit me a lot: Lester played such a little amount of guitar, he wasn't worth a s—t, if you'll excuse the expression, unless you got him at 90 miles an hour like that," Scruggs said of Flatt's playing on "Foggy Mountain Breakdown." "Yeah, if it was 90 miles an hour, he was at home with that."

Many fans and skilled players think the world of Flatt's guitar playing, even with its occasional eccentricities. Following an early reading of this material at the International Bluegrass Music Association's 2014 World of Bluegrass, banjoist Alan Munde offered spirited praise of Flatt's musicianship during a question-and-answer period. In 2008, guitarist Chris Sharp put online a video instruction method explaining Flatt's guitar-playing, which reveals some unexpected complexity. For instance, Flatt sometimes started a measure by hitting both a bass note and a downstroke across several strings with his thumb, then alternating finger and thumb to create a rolling pattern.[3]

Filling out the "Foggy Mountain Breakdown" session, Howard Watts pumped quarter notes on the acoustic bass, emphasizing the E minor chords by usually staying on an E note for three measures each time through the 16 bars. (Later generations of players and even the Foggy Mountain Boys tended to play the E minor chord for a more symmetrical two measures.) Seckler struck the characteristic bluegrass mandolin "chop," a percussive offbeat created by hitting a closed chord strongly, then lifting his fingers to mute it. Sims provided a smooth sustain as the banjo crackled on. Overall, the recording seems to capture the way a band can rise to new levels of energy when they have recently learned a hard-hitting tune.

The striking characteristic of the melody Tim O'Brien refers to is the repetition of the E minor chord, as Scruggs initially slows down the pattern of his roll to hit the chord one note at a time. As old-time tunes such as "Lonesome Road Blues" or "Going Down this Road Feeling Bad" stretch out a blues structure to return twice to the IV chord (such as C in the key of G), "Foggy Mountain Breakdown" includes two sections of E minor per 16-measure verse.

The composition is built on technique and on several distinct strains. Although some have made the case that banjo tunes don't really possess melodies—that they are all about tonality, sound, rhythm, and chords— "Foggy Mountain Breakdown" has a melody that made it a hit. In fact, it actually contains four distinct sections played by Scruggs, as well as the long-bowed fiddle solos rendered by Benny Sims.

Scruggs repeated sections in "Foggy Mountain Breakdown," but in the version he recorded on December 11, 1949, each of the 13 repetitions had something to distinguish it, as Atlanta five-string picker and collector Greg Earnest pointed out to me. Even during the fiddle breaks, Scruggs played such active backup that his notes remained distinct.

The first time through "Foggy Mountain Breakdown," Scruggs started hitting captivating licks right away, slurring a bluesy, flatted C-sharp on his B string and then hitting the open first, or D string, just a half tone apart. He was employing one of his rolls, or right-hand patterns, using the thumb both to play melody and to hit drone notes on the banjo's open fifth string, the one that runs only partway down the neck. His first and middle fingers alternate back and forth between picking melody and keeping the sixteenth notes flying.

"He had this impeccable timing, number one," Dobro virtuoso Jerry Douglas said of Scruggs. "That was the first thing for me. He had the kind of timing that you never hear anybody play with anymore.

"When he comes back in to take the next solo, it's like hydroplaning. He's got just a little bit of forward lean on it. He's so far on the front edge, he's on the precipice, but he never goes over, he never jumps."[4]

After rolling through four bars in G, Scruggs began the chord progression that set the tune apart from "Blue Grass Breakdown" and the bluegrass of the day. Bringing the middle finger of his left hand down on the first fret of the low D string and then sliding to the second fret, he started a string of four eighth notes spelling out the E minor chord, a slower-paced roll that soon doubled in time on the same chord. Then it was back to G again, this time punctuated with a flatted-third tone, the blues companion to the flatted five.

After repeating the E minor and G bars, Scruggs rolled into the notes of a G chord while the band hit a big D chord, the one classical musicians would call the dominant in this key. Then all returned to the tonic, or melodic home base.

(The original recording is heard in G-sharp because the musicians tuned their instruments up a half step, a technique designed to increase punch and brightness of sound, according to banjo picker and scholar Peter Wernick in "Masters of the Banjo.")

The second time through, Scruggs mostly reemphasized the basic tune, though there were variations in the way he moved back and forth between the E minor, and G chords.

Said Greg Earnest: "According to the Scruggs book, the first and second times through are repeats, but that's not quite true. Scruggs hits an open fourth string in one of the E minor chords the second time through. It may well have been a mistake, but I've always loved the way that growling low D note drops into the middle of the E minor chord."

The note that Earnest pointed out occurs about 18 seconds into the recording. It's so fleeting that it took me several repetitions to catch it. That Earnest heard it and analyzed its significance shows the degree of attention that hard-core Scruggs followers place on his every note. The D note very briefly creates an E minor seventh chord, an atypical voicing for bluegrass. Earnest continued: "Hearing it as the lowest note in the chord has always sounded ominous to me, especially when laid on top of the dissonance that's already going on with everybody playing E minor except for Flatt playing an E major."[5]

The memorable third chorus includes what Scruggs later called the un-intentional excerpt of a few bars from the patriotic tune "Columbia, the Gem of the Ocean." Scruggs often omitted this motif in later years, but it was a favorite with musicians such as Foggy Mountain Boy Josh Graves, who used to include it in his Dobro solos. In later years, Jerry Douglas also played the figure when accompanying Scruggs. Banjo innovator Béla Fleck has included it in his renditions of "Foggy Mountain Breakdown."

Sims started the fourth section, his first solo, with slower-paced figures, using double stops on the fiddle's lower strings, almost as though he was warming up. When the second half of the fiddle solo came along, he moved up the neck, riding high as the band churned along behind him.

By the sixth time through, Scruggs started to illustrate his command of chord positions higher up the banjo neck. This ability to play the same chord in several different positions set him apart from most country players of the era, although the "classic" banjo players also used more of the neck. He used the higher chord inversion to bend the bluesy B-flat note and contrast it to a D note on the top string. The E minor sections were also displayed in a higher position.

The seventh time through, Scruggs moved up the neck even farther before retreating to lower pitches for more variations on the E minor sections. By section eight, it was time to reprise "Columbia, the Gem of the Ocean," which must have been in the back of his mind that day. Section nine repeated portions of section six but ended with quick alternations between the second and third fret on the G string.

Bluegrass recordings going back to "Blue Grass Breakdown" had featured three and sometimes four lead instruments, but not "Foggy Mountain Breakdown." The only soloists were Scruggs and Sims, who reappeared to lead section 10 with some higher-pitched double stops. Scruggs's love for backup playing extended not only to vocalists, but also to instrumental soloists. He was never too far back in the mix of "Foggy Mountain Breakdown," rolling away during both halves of Sims's second set of solos, sections 10 and 11. Scruggs backed up the fiddle so emphatically that the Sims segments sound more like duets than solos. But these duets worked to great effect.

In section 12, Scruggs went back up the neck, emphasizing the bent third tone against the fifth and coming up with more variations for the E minor sections.

By the thirteenth time around, after more than two minutes of all-out picking by the entire crew, Scruggs went back to his main theme, the 16 measures that trademarked this banjo tune and helped establish the banjo itself as an essential element of bluegrass. The recording ended with a version of the commonplace "shave and a haircut" figure or tag that appears on fiddle recordings as early as Grayson and Whitter's 1928 version of "Sally Gooden."

Scruggs seems never to have noted an exact date on which he wrote "Foggy Mountain Breakdown." However, the dates of some related incidents give a likely window for the composition of sometime between February or March 1948 and September 1949, when J. D. Crowe recalled hearing it at a Flatt and Scruggs performance in Lexington. Scruggs noted that he didn't have "anything of his own" to play during his last appearance with Monroe, on the Opry's national radio segment. Clearly, he couldn't claim "Blue Grass Breakdown," a tune with Monroe's name on the copyright. In the interim, Scruggs had gone back to North Carolina, formed the band with Flatt and played dozens of dates with the evolving Foggy Mountain Boys.

Fiddler Sims said that Scruggs likely came up with "Foggy Mountain Breakdown" as something strong and lively to play as a banjo showcase. "That was the first instrumental that Lester and Earl ever recorded," Sims said. "It was actually just one of those pieces that Earl worked up to play on stage." Sims also recalled that Scruggs had another tune, initially titled "Pickin' and Tunin'," that eventually took on the name "Earl's Breakdown." That piece at first featured Scruggs simply using his ear and twisting a tuning peg to create the falling and ascending notes that formed the song's hook.

"That was before he had those special tuners put on his banjo," Sims said, referring to Scruggs's mechanical invention that allowed him more easily to change the pitch of strings for songs such as "Earl's Breakdown" and "Randy Lynn Rag."[6] This device made use of both his musical ear and his skill with machines.

Tunes like these gave Scruggs more prominence within the band. Instead of a traditional tune such as "Sally Goodin" or "Cumberland Gap," Scruggs could play his own work to get the audience going. It would make some money, too, if it got recorded.

The tune's name arose naturally enough, as the band had been called the Foggy Mountain Boys since its inception, after the Carter Family song, "Foggy Mountain Top." But what about "breakdown?" I asked him.

"Well, they just call a fiddle tune a fiddle tune, but it's a breakdown also," Scruggs said. "Just an up-tempo tune with no words to it. Just like 'Orange Blossom Special,' that's a breakdown tune."

Both scholars and fiddlers have equated the terms "hoedown" and "breakdown" to fast-paced showcases that might accompany dancers. American folklore scholar and fiddle historian Louie W. Atteberry wrote, "If today's 'Flint Hill Special' and 'Foggy Mountain Breakdown' are representative, the present notion of a breakdown or hoedown features strong rhythm, a driving banjo or banjo-fiddle lead, and speedy execution, appropriate for clogging, but probably too fast for a square dance."[7]

The term "breakdown" shows up in reference to a raucous party in a source as notable as *The Adventures of Huckleberry Finn*.[8]

In the pre-bluegrass repertoire, fiddle tunes such as "Billy in the Lowground" and "Temperance Reel" contained melodies that reflected relative minor chords, but Monroe and the first generation of bluegrass artists had yet to make use of them when recording. As with anything concerning Scruggs, the E minor chord in "Foggy Mountain Breakdown" can still spark a conversation. That's what happened at the Country Music Hall of Fame in Nashville, where a visitor can look behind glass and see "The Banjo" that Earl Scruggs used on "Foggy Mountain Breakdown," Bill Monroe's F-5 Gibson mandolin, Lester Flatt's D-28 and Maybelle Carter's Gibson L-5 archtop guitar, all in one exhibit. It's a display that sums up much of country string music's origins.

In the museum one day to see these instruments and other exhibits, I ran into John Hedgecoth, the picker and banjo expert. I told him I was writing about Earl Scruggs and "Foggy Mountain Breakdown."

"Where did the E minor come from?" Hedgecoth asked right away. Listeners can recognize the E minor chord in the moodier series of notes that Scruggs plays after the first four measures of the tune. The song and its chord changes are now so familiar that it takes mind travel to get even a sense of its groundbreaking nature at the time.

In 2007, Scruggs tried to recall why he had used the relatively rare E minor chord in 1949. "I don't know. It's been so long," he said. "But it'd just give you a tune with a distinct sound to it, to do that minor thing. There just wasn't many tunes that had a minor chord in it. And it just fit in with that tune real well, I thought."

The chord receives special emphasis when Scruggs varies the speed of his notes to about half the pace of the opening rolls in G.

"I deliberately stayed off the roll in spots, to keep it from sounding like hens scratching all the way through," he said. "It kind of gave it a variety of sounds, a little bit of, 'The band's going good. I'll just kind of jump around a little.'

"That doesn't really explain it. I don't read music so I can't describe it in any terms of the music."

In the recordings of the classic band with Monroe, Flatt, and Scruggs, there's almost no use of the relative minor chord that set "Foggy Mountain Breakdown" apart. It's still exciting and striking to hear, but in 1949 the chord was virtually unprecedented in the kind of hillbilly music that became bluegrass.

In the records that Bill Monroe's band made in the classic years, there's one intriguing feint to a minor chord. The Monroe composition "I'm Travelin' On and On," recorded in 1948, contains an unaccompanied vocal passage clearly using a relative minor as a passing chord. It comes as the rapid-fire gospel tune goes to half-time. With the instruments dropping out, the Blue Grass Quartet sings a relative minor on the word "my" on the repeat of the lyrics "my journey." It's brief and subtle.

Monroe often used minor chords in his later compositions and recordings. Some performances of the spiritual tune "Wayfaring Stranger" shifted back and forth between major and minor. Monroe sang and played it in what seemed to be a distinct A minor setting, then shifted to A major for the chorus for a striking, ghostly effect. He speculated in an interview with the historian Charles Wolfe as to why minor chords were seldom used in the early days of bluegrass.

"Bluegrass is a music that's really polished up," Monroe said. "You take pains with it, and if there's a G you're playing in and it needs to go in another chord, you go there today with it. Where maybe back years ago, they didn't hear that, and a lot of times there was minors and they never would go to it because they never did know how to make a minor chord."[9]

It's impossible to prove Monroe's contention that guitarists of the day didn't know how to make minor chords. Instruments including fiddle, mountain dulcimer, and fretless banjo played tonalities that would be considered minor modes today. However, several recorded examples show that some guitarists did not employ minor chords, even when, according to modern ears, the music seemed to call for it. One example comes from the January 22, 1935, recording of "Blackberry Blossom," by Fiddlin' Arthur Smith, with the Dixieliners—Alton Delmore on guitar and brother Rabon on tenor guitar—recorded in New Orleans for the Bluebird label. The melody notes in the second section clearly would fit right into a relative minor chord, and virtually any musician today accompanies that section of the tune with an E minor in the key of G. But the Delmores, accomplished musicians, play a plainly audible E major that creates an unsettling clash to modern ears. It has a certain appeal, a weird incongruity. And that same major-minor conflict shows up in the classic recording of "Foggy Mountain Breakdown."

Scruggs laughed when asked in 2007 if Flatt had not played an E *major* chord during the 1949 recording session.

"Many of the time," Scruggs said. "He just could not . . . he needed G, C, and D, and he liked that well enough that he never learned another."

The difference between the most typical E minor and E major chords on the guitar comes in the use of the index finger of the left hand on the third, or G string. If the guitarist presses the string down on the first fret to produce a G-sharp, the E chord is major; leave that finger off and it's minor.

Scruggs recalled: "I said, 'That's it, just don't press that one string,' but he'd go right back to the major chord, and it got to sounding pretty good. It's wrong; it's the wrong note. It sounds different, so just let it ride."

Perhaps torn by different impulses, Flatt appears to switch between versions of the chord in the 1949 cut.

"That's right," Scruggs said. "'Oh, that's too difficult, to make it,'" he said, quoting Flatt.

The vagueness or contradictions with which musicians approached the minor and major keys in Scruggs's day had been a while in the making. In unaccompanied singing, or in fiddling, such questions need not be directly resolved. If only a melody is being expressed, the notes of the backing remain in the ear of the listener.

But as singers and fiddlers added other instruments, the contrasts became more apparent. Perhaps to the detriment of an "ancient," deep-country sound, the sharps and flats became more uniform.

One prominent example came in "Down in the Willow Garden," also known as "Rose Connelly," the mournful murder ballad recorded in 1947 by Monroe's brother Charlie and his country-music band the Kentucky Pardners. Charlie's use of the E minor chord can be compared to the 1927 version of the same tune by the influential duo Grayson and Whitter. They played and sang the sixth tone around which a relative minor is built, but harmonized it differently, with major chords.

Earlier in 1949, Flatt and Scruggs themselves had recorded their version of "Down the Road," which clearly contained an E minor. However, previous versions of the same song root, such as Uncle Dave Macon's "Over the Road I'm Bound to Go," and "Feather Bed" in a 1928 recording by Gus Cannon's Jug Stompers, either left the chord out entirely or only hinted at it.

Placing the Scruggs composition in a broader context, the huge western-themed pop hit "Ghost Riders in the Sky," written in a minor key, was everywhere on radio and in the movies starting in spring 1949, just half a year before Scruggs took "Foggy Mountain Breakdown" into the studio. And Hank Williams's version of Emmett Miller's "Lovesick Blues," with a prominent minor section, had become a major hit after Williams recorded it at the Herzog Recording Studio.

In the 1950s, the use of minor chords in bluegrass became common. A notable example was Ralph Stanley's 1954 banjo showcase number, "Hard Times," which, after some introductory picking, settles on an ABA structure, with sections in D major, B minor, and back to D major. Even, so, there's a major-minor conflict, as guitarist Charlie Cline's solos consistently hit an A-flat note during the B minor sections instead of a more characteristically minor-y G. Like Lester Flatt's E major in "Foggy Mountain Breakdown," it sounds great once you get used to it.

━━━

In addition to containing the E minor chord, "Foggy Mountain Breakdown" stands out from many other fiddle and banjo tunes in having essentially only one section. The most common structure, especially for fiddle tunes, is AABB, or an introductory theme played twice, then a second strain, also repeated. "Foggy Mountain Breakdown" has no second strain. That means that it stays relentlessly in its flow of repeated chords and figures, creating charging excitement, just as the E minor chord gives what was then an exotic sound to the instrumental.

The musical information and innovation in "Foggy Mountain Breakdown" add up to a whole that hits harder than its relatively simple ingredients. One key is the bluegrass approach to tempo known as "drive," the characteristic that the actor and budding producer Warren Beatty cited, amid the intensity of the 1960s, when he settled on "Foggy Mountain Breakdown" as the musical hook of the movie *Bonnie and Clyde*. Scruggs's right-hand drive is key to the unflagging, almost mystical attachment banjo expert Jim Mills has felt to the 1949 performance.[10]

"The intensity with which he played it all the way through—it wasn't like there was one good break or the last break was good," Mills said. "It was continuous, it was all the way through, his right hand was like a jackhammer. And it wasn't just the banjo. A lot of people get hung up on one sound or whatever they're interested in, but the whole band was great.

"I told him one time, 'If y'all had taken a break or gone out for five minutes to get a breath of fresh air and came back in, it might not have come out like that.' It was like everything was right, the bass was right on the money, the mandolin chops, Benny Sims's fiddle—everything was just screaming, it was so good."

For Mills, the 1949 recording holds such appeal that he'll stop and listen to it all the way through whenever he encounters it. That's true, he has often said, even if "Foggy Mountain Breakdown" is coming from an 8-inch speaker in a truck-stop ceiling during a late-night visit from a tour bus. The recording holds the same fascination for many of the better players of the day, he said.

"He never played it to that same level again, in my opinion," Mills said. "It was like a life-or-death thing. It was like he killed it; it was just unbelievable from beginning to end."

10

THE NUMBER-ONE
BANJO PLAYER

In 1948 Bill Monroe had told a departing Flatt and Scruggs that the only way they could return to the Opry stage would be to rejoin the Blue Grass Boys. Monroe's opposition meant that for years they would lack the coast-to-coast coverage of Opry station WSM's 50,000-watt signal. Instead, they played stints at regional stations such as WVLK in Versailles, Kentucky; WCYB in Bristol in 1948 and in a return stint in 1950; and at WDAE in Tampa, Florida By 1953, they once again were being heard over WSM radio, though not on the Opry.

Through the second half of the 1950s, elements leading to another level of stardom came together for the band—the right record company, repertoire, songwriting, performance, band lineup, presentation, publicity, and business operation. By mid-decade, Louise Scruggs was managing the band from the family home on Donna Drive in the Nashville suburb of Madison.

By 1960 they would be "observed of all observers," as Ophelia remarked of Hamlet, at least in the country-bluegrass field. Also during the decade, Scruggs's fame spread as highly focused followers tried to learn his banjo style. These musicians, many of them amateurs, practiced for thousands of hours to approach the fluidity, style, and grace that he had brought to the five-string. His new compositions and techniques lit a beacon for others to follow as Scruggs, chiefly on his own, increased the world's supply of five-string banjos and players.

The earliest converts were players from Scruggs's part of the world, pickers who heard him first with Bill Monroe and then with Flatt and Scruggs, on live shows, radio, and records. However, musicians such as Roger Sprung in New York City and Mike Seeger in Baltimore and Washington, D.C., also got the urge to learn the Scruggs banjo style. Some, like Seeger, had gravitated to bluegrass after first favoring earlier forms of string music. Sprung still showed up at Southern fiddle contests into the 2010s, with banjos and books to market and bluegrass picking sessions to oversee.

"Foggy Mountain Breakdown" played a role in the increased popularity Flatt and Scruggs enjoyed in the 1950s. Its initial release didn't make the limited *Billboard* charts for country music, which contained a floating number of top discs, usually only about eight. Hank Williams's "Long Gone Lonesome Blues" dominated the airwaves, but "Foggy Mountain Breakdown" continued to draw new listeners. The tune was popular enough that concert posters for a Flatt and Scruggs show from the period billed the entire evening as "The Foggy Mountain Breakdown." An account of a 1959 banjo contest at a Pennsylvania music park, described by Mike Seeger in the folk newsletter *Gardyloo*, included "Foggy Mountain Breakdown" as a contest entry. Less than 10 years after the release of Scruggs's first instrumental, about a quarter of the contest's competitors played tunes written by or associated with him.

It took several years of hard work and relentless touring for Flatt and Scruggs to achieve a slightly easier and more rewarding career. They had appeared during the 1940s in radio markets that centered on states close to their native homes: North Carolina, South Carolina, Tennessee, Kentucky, and Virginia. Seeking their first radio base outside their home regions, the band ventured to Florida but found the state's market for bluegrass lacking in size and enthusiasm. Both the climate and the business scene proved unhealthy for the Foggy Mountain Boys, Curly Seckler remembered wryly.

"Lester said, 'I'll tell you one thing—one place down there, if you left the windows halfway up, the mosquitoes, the big ones couldn't get in,'" Seckler said. "That's all we ever had at show dates down there, was mosquitoes."[1]

=====

The hard times for the band during their tenure in Florida grew worse with the onset of Hurricane King in mid-October 1950. They managed not only to emerge intact from the storm but also to create a body of high-quality recordings while virtually in the midst of it. Their drive to succeed was to pay off in the form of some great, evolving music and a more permanent base in Nashville and on the Grand Ole Opry.

However, they first had to deal with Hurricane King, a Category 4 in today's terms. The storm killed three people in Florida and caused $281 million in damage in today's dollars.[2]

Producer Murray Nash recalled the band's reaction: "There were hurricane warnings, and they were getting out of there. They didn't want any part of that.

"I said, 'Well, where are you going?'

"'I don't know, but we're going to get out of here.'

"I said, 'Well, how do you know that the hurricanes aren't going to be where you're going, and not be here?'"

The Foggy Mountain Boys wanted to hightail it to points north, but Nash advised a different course, one that would solve two problems. The act had asked to leave Mercury Records and the label had agreed, under the condition that they record the number of sides specified during the original three-year term of their contract. With the hurricane on the way, Nash said, why not retreat to the safety of radio station WDAE, families in tow, and record the required tunes while the hurricane passed? WDAE, affiliated with the *Tampa Daily Times*, was located in the newspaper's downtown building at 114 North Franklin Street, a stout former bank that dated to the 1880s.[3]

"We had to cut 14 or 15 numbers for them before we could go on Columbia Records," Seckler recalled. "We cut them in the studio down there while there was a hurricane outside."

———

Scruggs and partners showed their usual professionalism during the sessions of October 20, 1950. The lineup was the same as the "Foggy Mountain Breakdown" crew, except that Mount Airy, North Carolina–born musician Charles Johnson, dubbed "Little Jody Rainwater" by Flatt, assumed bass duties from the unrelated Howard Watts, known as "Cedric Rainwater" during stints with Hank Williams and Flatt and Scruggs. Johnson took a guest turn on mandolin for the session's first tune, the lovely, mournful "Cora is Gone."

Two Flatt and Scruggs standards, "Roll in My Sweet Baby's Arms" and "Salty Dog Blues," had their first recordings that day, as well as two widely played Scruggs-led instrumentals, "Pike County Breakdown" and "Farewell Blues." The hard-driving "Pike County Breakdown" was a Bill Monroe composition that dated from Flatt and Scruggs's tenure with the Blue Grass Boys. However, Flatt and Scruggs's version was released before Monroe's, which essentially became a cover of his own tune.[4]

With its rollicking tempo and melody highlighting the bluesy flatted seventh tone of the scale, it has become a standard for banjo pickers and fiddlers alike. Benny Sims's fast, accurate work on the piece represents much more confident fiddling than on "Foggy Mountain Breakdown."

As for "Farewell Blues," it was the first recording of Scruggs's several expeditions into noncountry tunes and chord changes, revealing an adventuresome approach to repertoire that would mark the rest of his career. A product of pop composers Elmer Schoebel, Paul Mares, and Leon Roppolo, the tune was recorded in 1922 by the Friars Society, later known as the New Orleans Rhythm Kings. It reemerged in versions by Benny Goodman, Glenn Miller, Django Reinhardt, Count Basie, and many others. The timing of those releases meant the tune was all over the radio during the years when young Earl Scruggs was always listening for something with a melody.

"I listened to anything that had a tune to it, yeah," he told me in 2007. "Even if it was orchestra. I'd listen to it, if they played it to where I could tell [the melody].

"You know, some of them was a 10- or 15-piece orchestra and . . . no one taking a good lead, so . . . it all kind of washes along together. But yeah, I liked everything if I could follow along with the tune."

In the 1950 recording of "Farewell Blues," Scruggs not only followed the tune, but also added some twists of his own, including an eccentric D-flat note in a C7 chord during his last solo. Joti Rockwell, an associate professor of music and musicology at Pomona College, describes the note as creating a "G diminished triad over the underlying tonic C major harmony." Just a half-step above the tone on which the song rests, it's a "wild" note that would work in the bebop jazz musical vocabulary. It's also a musical cousin to Lester Flatt's E major chord on "Foggy Mountain Breakdown," where Flatt was hitting the note just a half tone above the note on which the song is based. Scruggs surely knew he was playing an "off" note and liked the sound of it, just as he liked the E minor/E major contrast in "Foggy Mountain Breakdown."

Less than a year earlier, "Foggy Mountain Breakdown" had been the first instrumental recorded by the act, but it soon had company in the Scruggs repertoire with a string of memorable compositions and adaptations. There was plenty of material ahead to feed the growing masses of his followers.

The mid-1950s also brought several landmarks in the band's history. The leaders hired Burkett (Uncle Josh) Graves to play Dobro and Paul Warren to play fiddle. And they joined the Grand Ole Opry under the sponsorship of the Martha White flour company.

Warren, a veteran of Johnny and Jack's band with a deep store of old-time tunes, was to provide skilled, energetic playing for Flatt and Scruggs as long as they remained co-bandleaders. He also offered a lively stage presence and pitched in on bass vocals.

Graves is known as the first Dobro player to move from a two-finger picking style to the three-finger roll, a change that spread Scruggs's technique even farther. Even his right-hand tools, a thumb pick and one finger pick, had to change to match the style. "Earl gave him another finger pick," said Jerry Douglas, a longtime pal of Graves. "He said, 'You're going to need this.'"

In interviews that appeared in Fred Bartenstein's book *Bluegrass Bluesman*, Graves talked about the discipline that Scruggs brought to the Foggy Mountain Boys' ensemble sound. Both Graves and Scruggs tended to play strings of sixteenth notes, a mix that could get cacophonous if Graves didn't vary his timing to stay out of Scruggs's way, or vice versa.

"Earl would really put the pressure on me, and sometimes I knew our rolls would clash, so I'd go another way," Graves said. "He was teaching me then, and I can still feel them eyes on me if I did it wrong. He wouldn't say nothing—just look at me. I had to figure a way to get around that banjo. Listen to the records and you'll know we never played over each other. He'd go one way and I'd go another. I guess that's what made it so clean."

Adding Graves into the Foggy Mountain Boys meant, crucially, that they sounded less and less like Monroe and the Blue Grass Boys. The blues-drenched Dobro, when melded with the banjo and fiddle, kept them closer to the growing rock 'n' roll movement than most bluegrass bands.

Flatt and Scruggs's connection to the Martha White organization drove their move to Nashville. The flour company dated to 1899 and bore the name of the founder Richard Lindsey's daughter.[5] The Martha White company became a mover and shaker in country music after Cohen Williams bought it in 1941 and started sponsoring segments on WSM and the Opry. Flatt and Scruggs started out on the 5:45 a.m. radio slot and then moved to the Opry cast under Martha White's sponsorship in 1955, despite Bill Monroe's opposition.

According to Graves, Monroe and others signed a petition to keep Flatt and Scruggs off the Saturday Night Opry.

"Cohen told them, 'Well, it's either my boys do that show or I drop all the advertisement I've got on WSM,'" Graves said. "That was $250,000 to $300,000 a year. They ain't going to let that go, you know. So we started doing 8 to 8:30 on Saturday night, and then they switched us to 10 to 10:15 or 10:30 to quarter to eleven, I forget which. And son, anywhere you'd go you'd hear 'Martha White!'"

As Flatt and Scruggs's Opry performances, records and live shows—even their commercials—spread their sound, a raft of young players were to grow up fascinated with Scruggs's speed, style, and artistry. Their performances of Scruggs's tunes became another means of spreading his name and the reputation of the band.

In the early years, Scruggs himself was a principal resource for players out to learn his style, showing a lifelong sense of fellowship and generosity that dated to his days as a Blue Grass Boy. The incident after an Opry show falls out of this chronology but shows Scruggs's generosity from his first days in the spotlight.

"I hadn't been with Monroe very long; there was a guy from somewhere in Virginia—seemed like around Salem, Virginia—came and came back and stayed around," Scruggs said in 2007. "And he asked me a bunch of questions about the banjo. And I'd talk to him. Anyway, he wanted to know what was I doing tomorrow, Sunday. And he said he wanted to know if he could come up and spend a day with me, or part of the day, and I said sure."

History does not record the identity of the early adopter, but Scruggs remembered that he lived at the Tulane Hotel in Nashville, where Scruggs stayed when not on the road. As he would with Ralph Stanley, Scruggs took the time to teach the visiting musician some elements of his method.

"The reason I remember it so well," said Scruggs, "Monroe was standing over not far from us. Soon as the visitor went out, Monroe said, 'You don't want to fool with that boy.' And I said, 'Why?' He said, 'All he wants to do is steal your stuff.'

"'Steal my stuff? What do you mean steal?'

"'Well, he just wants to pick like you.'

"I said, 'S—t, hurray for that. If he's confused about it, something I do, if he'll ask me, I'll show him. I can't teach; I'll show him.'"[6]

Throughout the 1950s, and indeed into the 2000s, Scruggs heard from budding pickers from all over and reached out in turn whenever he could.

═══

During the '50s, the Foggy Mountain Boys had myriad strengths in addition to Scruggs's banjo. However, according to record man Murray Nash, it was Scruggs who pushed the act's record sales up to high levels.

"Of course, the main thing musically that they relied on was Scruggs's banjo playing," Nash told the Country Music Foundation's John Rumble. "He was the greatest. He was the number-one banjo player. Of course, when you've got the number one in your pocket, you're going to sell records with it."

Despite their success at Mercury, the act decided to move on to Columbia. The label change, according to Nash, reflected the increasingly important role that music publishing played in Nashville and the business at large.

Recording artists got paid for the sales of their records in what are called mechanical royalties. Publishing royalties went to the song's composer and publisher, both for record sales and for airplay, the latter called performance royalties. For some bands and artists, publishing provided a more dependable stream of revenue than touring and record sales.

When Flatt and Scruggs were on Mercury, the label was not involved in their publishing. "I had no written contract song-wise, and I didn't have their songs, actually," Nash said. "I didn't publish any of their songs. Their songs were already published when we recorded them."

When Troy Martin entered the Flatt and Scruggs saga, he was in his late 30s and had a long career in vaudeville, radio, and records behind him. "Ex-band leader Troy Martin is repping Peer International property in Nashville," *Billboard* said.[7] That meant Martin was working for the powerful Peer publishing empire, which had published the songs of both Bill Monroe and Flatt and Scruggs. But in addition to plugging tunes for the publishing pioneer Ralph Peer, Martin also served as a talent scout for Columbia Records Nashville chief Don Law.[8]

Don Law's career defies a thorough telling in this space. But roughly a decade earlier, he had assured himself a place in world music history as the producer of every song recorded by Mississippi bluesman Robert Johnson, one of a handful of essential American roots artists. He also cut key recordings with western swing king Bob Wills and his Texas Playboys, among countless others.

Flatt and Scruggs signed with Columbia Records in 1950. The company would be their label until they split in 1969, and Law their producer until 1967. Law was a skilled studio veteran, and much memorable music came from this connection.

For several years in the 1950s, Flatt and Scruggs profited from having recordings released by two thriving labels. For fans and record stores, that meant "Earl's Breakdown" and "Flint Hill Special" were arriving from Columbia as Mercury continued to sell "Foggy Mountain Breakdown" and to release additional Scruggs performances such as "Farewell Blues." (Mercury had squirreled away the products of the Tampa sessions for future release.)

Murray Nash blamed Troy Martin for luring Flatt and Scruggs to Columbia, implying that Martin's desire to secure their publishing for Peer International was the reason. However, Lester Flatt and Earl Scruggs already published their songs through Peer, so it's hard to pin down the reason for the shift.

"So why couldn't Troy Martin have just simply picked up the songs and let them continue on Mercury?" the Country Music Foundation's John Rumble asked in 1983.

"You would have to have asked Troy that, I guess," Nash said. (Martin had died in 1977.)

According to Neil V. Rosenberg's liner notes for the Bear Family CD set *Flatt & Scruggs 1948–1959*, "Troy Martin would eventually place many songs recorded by Flatt and Scruggs not only with Peer, but also with other publishing companies.[9] Some of these bore Martin's name as one of the writers, suggesting that Martin had perhaps had his eye on the duo's publishing all along.

Flatt and Scruggs continued to vary their circuit and types of media, showing up on September 13, 1954, for 24 performances on Broadway in a stage version of the Old Dominion Barn Dance at the 48th Street Theatre. Among a cast that also included Sunshine Sue and Joe Maphis, they performed what critic John Chapman called "way back mountain music."[10] They would return to New York City in 1961 with an Opry troupe at Carnegie Hall and eventually score a hit live album at the same venue in 1962.

In addition, their syndicated Grand Ole Opry–branded Martha White show was airing in more than 100 markets, the beginning of mass-media exposure that would leave the rest of the bluegrass field behind. Other bluegrass artists had broad exposure on radio, and some went on to act as hosts or guests on syndicated television shows. But Flatt and Scruggs not only outpaced others in the number of stations carrying their TV show, but they also went on to appearances on numerous network television shows and eventually heard their music gain significant exposure in movies, most notably in *Bonnie and Clyde*.

As the '50s progressed, bluegrass experienced growth among fans and musicians even though the field as yet had no *Bluegrass Unlimited*, no International Bluegrass Music Association, no "bluegrass in the classroom" programs, no websites or blogs, no bluegrass tours of the tropics. Before it was generally known as bluegrass, the style attracted thousands of dedicated, adventurous banjo pickers. Scruggs became a role model because he played with melody, speed, and dexterity, in the style he developed himself, while placing high values on accurate time and perfectly rounded tone. His example led other pioneering bluegrass banjoists first to play as he did, then to innovate, as he also had done.

Banjo was a key element for the Virginia-born brother duo of Ralph and Carter Stanley, who angered Monroe by recording his version of "Molly and Tenbrooks" before he could release it. The Stanleys were making music that still stands among the best mountain-style bluegrass of all time. Ralph had grown up around his mother's energetic down-picking banjo, which he later revived with performances of tunes such as "Shout Little Lulie." But by the time he started recording with Carter as the Stanley Brothers, he used a two-finger right-hand approach that echoed what he heard in acts such as Mainer's Mountaineers, where Wade Mainer's banjo was featured.

Ralph Stanley got some up-close attention from Scruggs just after Flatt and Scruggs left Monroe. However, David W. Johnson's notable Stanley Brothers biography *Lonesome Melodies* presents a different, or at least an additional, version of Ralph Stanley's five-string education.[11]

In Johnson's account from an unnamed band member, Carter locked Ralph in a room with his banjo and recordings of Scruggs, "ordering Ralph to play in the Scruggs style." Although perhaps apocryphal, the story shows how deeply Scruggs's playing had embedded itself into the expanding bluegrass style.

When he was urged to learn three-finger picking, Stanley took the Scruggs style and ran with it, while developing a distinctive approach. In his adaptation of the basic three-finger roll, he tended to play melody with his index finger instead of emphasizing notes with the thumb of his right hand, as Scruggs did. Stanley was one of the earliest banjo pickers to take Scruggs-style banjo and give it his own imprint, using a right-on-time rhythmic approach that was graceful and driving at once. In Ralph Stanley's recordings, we likely hear the first of the many variations on Scruggs's style that were to enliven banjo playing for decades to come.

Two more brother teams, Jim and Jesse McReynolds and Bobby and Sonny Osborne, were also gathering steam and creating individual takes on modern string music, although their recording careers didn't begin until the early 1950s. Sonny Osborne was a precocious Scruggs follower who threw himself into the style, practicing as much as 15 hours a day. That dedication earned him a job with Bill Monroe when he was 14 years old. During decades with the Osborne Brothers, Sonny remained true to Scruggs's style while adding elements of hard-country instrumental style and jazz. "He could play straight down the line Earl or step out into crazy, jazzy terrain without missing a beat," Tony Trischka said.[12]

Jim & Jesse had a number of notable banjo pickers, including Hoke Jenkins, whose place Scruggs had taken in the Morris Brothers band. The band member whose playing likely most defined their sound was Allen Shelton, a solid player who exemplified the elusive "bounce" that—to simplify greatly—slightly syncopates the Scruggs roll. In addition, by 1956 Shelton had approximated steel-guitar licks on the banjo in a recording of "Your Old Standby" with Jim Eanes.

Jimmy Martin, an East Tennessee boy who won fame as one of Monroe's finest duet partners, employed a long line of standout banjo players in his Sunny Mountain Boys. Martin's pickers had to adhere to his honky-tonk–influenced "Good 'n' Country" time. The best known of these banjo players was Kentuckian J. D. Crowe, who showed rock and r&b influences in his playing and later took a major role in reimagining bluegrass with his New South band. Crowe heard the Foggy Mountain Boys as a teenager and learned Scruggs's style early.

Interest in music not too different from bluegrass was also building in the urban Northeast. Musicians such as Pete Seeger were joining forces with roots giants Woody Guthrie, Lead Belly, Cisco Houston, Sonny Terry, and Brownie McGee in music that, like bluegrass, crossed genres and generations. Guthrie's 1946 "John Henry," with a driving tempo and whooping harmonica by North Carolina bluesman Terry, provided another example of musicians who mixed ingredients in powerful torrents of sound.

Pete Seeger was playing in a driving style derived from the playing of southern mountain players like Rufus Crisp, Samantha Bumgardner, and Bascom Lamar Lunsford, and was building general interest in the banjo. Seeger would eventually promote Scruggs-style three-finger playing in his influential instruction book. He was foundational to a folk movement that would eventually help bring banjo and bluegrass to listeners from outside the music's traditional base.

While the small crew of early bluegrass acts played grueling circuits of schoolhouses, radio stations, and country-music parks, a young Mike Seeger was pursuing music while working as a conscientious objector in a VA hospital. The half-brother of folk-music star and activist Pete Seeger and the child of musicologists Charles and Ruth Seeger, Mike Seeger was also to become one of the people most responsible for the spread of bluegrass and old-time music to new audiences.

In his Mike Seeger biography *Music from the True Vine*, Bill C. Malone recounts Seeger's 1950s excursions, carrying a tape recorder, to country-music parks not far from the Washington, D.C., area. At one such show in Maryland, Seeger heard Flatt and Scruggs, along with other acts, later calling the day "as near about to a religious experience as I have ever had." His epiphany was caused, he said, by hearing "music so powerful and musicianship so dazzling." Seeger was eventually much more closely associated with the pre-bluegrass traditional music known as "old-time" or "old-timey." But his first encounters with bluegrass had been riveting.[13]

Taking on a sideline career engineering radio and records, Seeger initiated two Folkways Records album projects that broke new ground. These long-playing records focused first on Scruggs-style banjo and then on bluegrass as a complete style. The first of these, released in 1957 as *American Banjo: Scruggs Style*, gathered recordings of pickers including Snuffy Jenkins, Larry Richardson, Scruggs's brother Junie, the pioneering female banjo player Roni Stoneman, and Mike Seeger himself. The project showed how deeply Earl Scruggs's style had ingrained itself into string-band music during the little more than 10 years since he was first heard on the Opry with Monroe. Clearly, the term "Scruggs style" was being widely adopted.

The second disc for Folkways Records—*Mountain Music Bluegrass Style*—chronicled the growing scene of musicians influenced by the founding acts: Monroe, Flatt and Scruggs, and the Stanley Brothers.

All of this was taking place in the context of the commercialized folk boom created by acts including the Kingston Trio, who mixed novelty tunes and calypso with pop ballads such as "Scotch and Soda." They also reworked folk songs such as their massive hit "Tom Dooley." The group's banjo man, Dave Guard, performed an odd but clearly Scruggs-influenced break on the popular tune "The MTA."

Both the Kingston Trio and Earl Scruggs performed at the first Newport Folk Festival, in 1959. Scruggs was backed by the journeyman bluegrass act Hylo Brown and the Timberliners. The event was an adaptation of the famed Newport Jazz Festival and brought acts such as a young Joan Baez to predominantly noncountry audiences who were tuning into what was being billed as authentic, indigenous music.

The appeal to noncountry audiences came as Flatt and Scruggs's long dedication to records, broadcast, and personal performances also started to pay off in a string of country chart appearances such as the 1959 release "Cabin on the Hill," a No. 9 record in *Billboard*.

Their popularity led to appearances such as the April 15, 1956, ABC-TV *Grand Ole Opry* broadcast with veteran stage and screen hoofer Buddy Ebsen. Soon to be known to millions of TV viewers as Jed Clampett of *The Beverly Hillbillies*, Ebsen in 1956 executed some creditable buck-dancing and square-dance rounds with Opry crew members including Minnie Pearl and Rod Brasfield.

"Yeah, boy! Mr. Ebsen, you've got talent, Buddy," Brasfield hollered. "Yes, sir, you're liable to go places in this business!"

Within a few years, Ebsen would inhabit the starring role in the television show that ushered Flatt, Scruggs, and the sounds of three-finger banjo into millions of American living rooms.

Earl Scruggs and the author socialize backstage at the historic Ryman Auditorium in Nashville. Photo by Dan Loftin courtesy XPress Photography.

The first release of "Foggy Mountain Breakdown" came on a 78 rpm Mercury Records disc in March 1950. Photo by Thomas Goldsmith.

Scruggs played a Gibson RB-11 banjo during his early tenure with Bill Monroe. Photo courtesy Jim Mills Collection.

Lester Flatt and Earl Scruggs were photographed on December 11, 1949, the day "Foggy Mountain Breakdown" was recorded. Photo courtesy Jim Mills Collection.

Flatt and Scruggs and the Foggy Mountain Boys spent most of 1952 performing at WPTF in Raleigh, North Carolina. Photo courtesy Marshall Wyatt Collection.

Flatt and Scruggs, who are decked out in gangster clothing reflecting themes of the hit movie *Bonnie & Clyde*, for which they provided the theme, "Foggy Mountain Breakdown." Photo courtesy Country Music Foundation.

Earl Scruggs, seated, formed the highly successful Earl Scruggs Revue in 1969, the same year he and Lester Flatt broke up their longstanding partnership. Standing in rear are Gary Scruggs, Josh Graves, Steve Scruggs, Jody Maphis, and Randy Scruggs.

In a photo shot in Boston in 1967, Scruggs plays an Earl Scruggs Vega banjo, a departure from the Mastertone on which he performed for decades. Photo courtesy Bluegrass Unlimited.

Sonny Osborne, an early practitioner of Scruggs-style picking, greets friends and fans at the 2016 Banjothon celebration. Photo by Thomas Goldsmith.

Curly Seckler, a member of the Foggy Mountain Boys band that recorded "Foggy Mountain Breakdown," reminisces in 2013 at his home outside Nashville. Photo by Thomas Goldsmith.

Jim Mills plays one of his prewar, original five-string Gibson Mastertone banjos in his showroom outside Raleigh, North Carolina. Photo by Thomas Goldsmith.

Life on the road with Flatt and Scruggs gets informal at Lake of the Ozarks, Missouri, in June 1967. Photo by Doc Hamilton.

11

THE BEVERLY HILLBILLIES
WELCOMES THE BANJO

By the early '60s, Earl Scruggs and his banjo had traveled hundreds of thousands of miles via two-lane roads, turnpikes, and airways. Flatt and Scruggs had journeyed back and forth between New York's Great White Way and California's country music scene, spreading their sound via schoolhouse shows, concert halls, and college auditoriums, as well as radio towers and television signals.

But when they showed up on a weekly television show that quickly grabbed tens of millions of viewers, it meant that the sound of Scruggs's Granada had met the mainstream of American pop culture. This increased television presence kicked off Flatt and Scruggs's years of greatest popularity and commercial success. However, the 1960s presented both opportunities and conflicts, forces that were to separate the duo for good.

The television show *The Beverly Hillbillies* was an unabashed cornball comedy on CBS. It became the top-rated television show for its first two seasons, 1962–1963 and 1963–1964. A listing of most-seen broadcast shows since the dawn of TV placed 13 episodes of the show in its Top 100.

Each of the show's 274 episodes featured the sound of Scruggs's banjo, playing the theme and other tunes during his appearances on the show with Flatt. West Coast vocalist Jerry Scoggins sang the theme's televised version, and various session players contributed incidental music. Seven episodes presented Lester Flatt and Earl Scruggs playing themselves, getting significant airtime for speaking roles and musical performances. Thrown into unlikely sitcom plots, the real-life musicians came across as levelheaded country folk, not yokels.

The cast featured such showbiz veterans as Buddy Ebsen and Irene Ryan, as well as such off-the-wall guests as ill-starred actor Sharon Tate and pinup star Joi Lansing. Tate didn't appear in any episodes with Flatt and Scruggs; the actress was two years away from her big role in *The Valley of the Dolls* and four years away from her death at the hands of the Manson family. Tate became just another of the oddly notable people—from Richard Nixon to Francois Truffaut, from Minnie Pearl to David Letterman—to intersect with Earl Scruggs's life orbit.

The Beverly Hillbillies certainly distracted and usually entertained the viewing public. Perpetually in reruns, the show can still bring forth belly laughs when seen half a century after its prime.

"Equal parts Steinbeck and absurdism, the nouveau riche-out-of-water Clampetts populated the top-rated program of their premier season, remained in the top ten throughout the rest of the decade, and had regular weekly episode ratings which rivaled those of Super Bowls," broadcast historian Paul Cullum wrote.[1]

The overwhelming popularity of a show like *The Beverly Hillbillies*, which ran until 1971, was possible because only three broadcast networks dominated television. Landing a prominent musical role and occasional guests spots on a top network show took Flatt and Scruggs far from their customary realms into a large share of the nation's small screens.

Country music had grown quickly as a commercial commodity in the 1920s as soon as radio and record executives discovered the audiences that felt at home with music by Eck Robertson, the Skillet Lickers, Jimmie Rodgers, the Carter Family, Charlie Poole, and others. Similarly, television, initially in syndicated shows, helped bluegrass and country performers bring their folksy sounds into people's homes. Acts could promote new songs and revive favorites, announce public appearances, and plug recent record releases.

Early regional performers included Ernie Lee at WLW in Cincinnati in 1947, Pee Wee King at WAVE in Louisville in 1948, and Lulu Belle and Scotty Wiseman at Chicago's WNBQ. "By 1956, almost 100 live local country and western shows aired on more than 80 stations in 30 states," according to the *Encyclopedia of Television*. Other networks' efforts were Red Foley's *Ozark Jubilee* on ABC from 1955–1961, the *Tennessee Ernie Ford Show* on NBC and ABC, from 1955–1965) and the CBS country music show hosted by Jimmy Dean.[2]

What became known as cross-promotion spread as performers like Pee Wee King, in a May 1950 advertisement in *Billboard*, hawked his regular appearances on Louisville, Kentucky, television station WAVE along with show dates and RCA releases such as "Bonaparte's Retreat."[3]

Bluegrass performers Jim & Jesse, Don Reno and Red Smiley, and the Stanley Brothers also adapted to the new medium on smaller outlets. Bill Monroe never starred in his own show, although he often appeared on Grand Ole Opry telecasts.

Flatt and Scruggs made their guest appearances on *The Beverly Hillbillies* as TV veterans, given their years of appearing on shows in a rotation of Southern cities. That grueling schedule came up in a 2009 interview of Scruggs by banjo players and authorities Béla Fleck and Tony Trischka. Fleck asked Scruggs about Malcolm Gladwell's often-cited theory that high levels of performance come after 10,000 hours of practice. Gladwell cited the Beatles, Steve Jobs, and Bill Gates as examples.

"There may be something to that," Scruggs said.

Fleck asked how much the band worked when really busy, when almost all their playing was on stage, not in practicing.

Scruggs replied: "Well . . . let's see, for a long time we'd work Augusta, Georgia, Monday; Atlanta, Tuesday; Florence, South Carolina, Wednesday; Huntington, West Virginia, Thursday; and Friday was Jackson, Tennessee; and WSM here—The Opry—on Saturday."

In addition to their syndicated show and *The Beverly Hillbillies*, Flatt and Scruggs appeared often on network variety shows and specials. In 1963 and 1964, they caught another crest of the folk revival with three appearances on the ABC series *Hootenanny*.

The noted folklorist Archie Green, then on the faculty at the University of Illinois at Champaign-Urbana, had an extended correspondence with Louise and Earl Scruggs in the latter half of the '60s. The topics ranged from his plans to bring Flatt and Scruggs to the University of Illinois for a major concert to origins of songs that the duo played. "I keep getting good reports from students who saw Earl and Lester on *The Beverly Hillbillies* last week,"

Green wrote Louise on February 12, 1963. "It is a source of satisfaction to any teacher when his students 'catch on.'"[4] Green was deeply involved with the university's 400-member Folksong Club, which brought both bluegrass and folk performers to campus, with Flatt and Scruggs appearing in 1962.

A show at the folk-based Ash Grove night club in Los Angeles convinced veteran Hollywood producer-writer Paul Henning that Flatt and Scruggs should pick and sing the *Beverly Hillbillies* theme song. Henning's visit likely came during the gig they played from November 21 through November 26, 1961. The extended date got an advance notice in the California Institute of Technology student newspaper from a budding bluegrass fan.[5]

By the early '60s, treks to the West Coast had become regular parts of the band's touring schedule. The shows weren't all for folky or bluegrass crowds. On November 9, 1961, the Chula Vista *Star-News* advertised an 11:30 p.m. "one only" performance at the Bostonia Ballroom in San Diego, a hard-country haven where the bluegrass was sandwiched in between dance-music sets by Smokey Rogers and Western Caravan. They appeared at the Hollywood Bowl on June 15, 1962, as part of a "Western Spectacular" with the Carter Family and others and returned to the Ash Grove in 1962.

When Henning caught the Foggy Mountain Boys at the Ash Grove, it was another instance in which their music and show, instead of a showbiz pitch, brought a bid to move onto higher ground. After initial resistance from Louise Scruggs, who thought the show would make a mockery of country people, the act agreed.

In an interview with *Emmy TV Legends*, Henning recalled the genesis for the show. It was based in part on his own youthful camping trips in rural Missouri, he said.

"If you could find someone from a remote, protected spot—you know, they didn't have radio, they didn't have television, telephone, anything—to transplant them by some means into a modern world, and that was the beginning of *The Beverly Hillbillies*.

"My first thought was New York. And I thought, this would mean expensive location trips and why not transplant them to Beverly Hills where you have the same sophistication—maybe more? And to make that possible, they somehow had to become affluent. And that's how Jed was out shooting at some food and 'up through the ground came a-bubbling crude.'

"And all of a sudden they are millionaires. There had been a musical group called The Beverly Hill Billies, and I didn't know any of them personally but this title stayed with me and it seemed so apt."[6]

The West Coast outfit called the Beverly Hill Billies had significant popularity in the 1930s, with a fun-poking version of country and cowboy music. Decades later, surviving members won a settlement from CBS over the network's use of their name.[7]

In retrospect it's striking to see how Henning's framing of the show premise echoed, in a telescoped fashion, the journey that Scruggs had made from nearly "starving out" at Flint Hill to approaching the Hollywood dream of swimming pools and movie stars. In line with one of our culture's deepest-held dreams, Scruggs and partner Flatt had moved from backwoods obscurity to the front of the line. The tossed-off description of Jed Clampett as a "poor mountaineer" who could barely feed his family sounded poignant in light of the Scruggs family's financial troubles after the death of George Elam Scruggs.

Otherwise, the *Hillbillies* theme song, written by Henning, survives as a witty exposition of the show's premise. It's driven by Scruggs's precise banjo, played with a more relaxed approach than the one heard in "Foggy Mountain Breakdown." But it highlights his tone, sense of timing, and ability to make the most of moments like the C-sharp passing tone, from C to D, that breaks up the otherwise standard tune. Scruggs's older son, Gary, recounted the progression of the tune from theme to hit record.

"Flatt and Scruggs recorded the music track for the song, which Jerry Scoggins sang, for the show's opening and closing," Gary Scruggs wrote me. "Soon after that recording, Mom suggested that Flatt and Scruggs rerecord the song with Lester singing for a single release on their label, Columbia Records.

"Flatt and Scruggs recorded it, and that F&S version soon became the Number One record on the country music charts, the only Number One record that F&S ever had. It was the first so-called 'bluegrass' song to go to Number One, and it also showed up in the pop charts as well."

It was a breakthrough for the act, outstripping the popularity they had built since 1948 on radio, records, and regional television. Gary Scruggs recalled that it even impressed people his age in the Nashville suburb of Madison, where the family lived.

"I came to know that people my age at that time were very aware of it, and it was a major factor in making me realize that Dad was not the 'typical' father who worked from 9 to 5," Gary wrote. "Up until then he was 'just Dad.'"

If the TV show was so important, why isn't this book about "The Ballad of Jed Clampett"? *The Beverly Hillbillies* and its theme song greatly widened the popularity of both Flatt and Scruggs and the five-string banjo. However, it didn't produce the deep-seated reaction—of blood and laughter flowing together—created by the use of the rapid-fire "Foggy Mountain Breakdown" in *Bonnie and Clyde*, one of the movies that most closely defined the '60s.

Karen Linn, author of *That Half-Barbaric Twang: The Banjo in American Popular Culture*, makes a convincing case that Scruggs not only created a familiar profile for himself on *The Beverly Hillbillies*, but that he also reworked the image of the banjo player for the large network audience. Flatt and Scruggs played "somewhat more dignified cousins" of the Clampetts," Linn wrote:

"Even though Earl Scruggs played the cousin of the Clampett family, the poker-faced virtuoso was not performing his music in the tradition of the minstrel-comedian."[8]

Linn compares Scruggs to Alfred Farland (1864–1954), known as the "Scientific Banjoist of Pittsburgh, Pa." Farland, she reports, refused to present a comedic image or wear a costume, choosing to emphasize his considerable technique.[9]

"But Earl Scruggs's innovation has proven to be of more lasting consequence than Farland's. Scruggs's imitators are legion forty-five years after his initial appearance with the Blue Grass Boys, and other bluegrass banjoists explain their innovations by comparison to 'classic' Scruggs style," Linn wrote.

Scruggs didn't need to exaggerate his country background: Both he and Flatt had lived the life that *The Beverly Hillbillies* portrayed in buffoonish references. The Clampett clan comically tried to keep up country ways in their oversized Los Angeles mansion, though Granny and Jed could display unexpected wiles when confronted with West Coast dishonesty or pretense. When Flatt and Scruggs showed up, playing themselves, they brought along an authentic country flavor, even while serving as straight men to the Clampetts' shticks.

Cross-promotion abounded, as in the November 20, 1968, episode "Bonnie, Flatt and Scruggs." It came at the height of popularity for the movie *Bonnie and Clyde*. The duo appeared in the episode in gangster attire, supposedly straight from filming a commercial. There was always time for a tune, as actress Joi Lansing, portraying "Gladys Flatt," noted as she attempted to learn country cooking from Granny in the mansion's kitchen.

"That's 'Foggy Mountain Breakdown,' the song they did for *Bonnie and Clyde*," Lansing said as the tune drifted in from an adjoining room in the mansion.

Said Irene Ryan as Granny: "Well, this time they're going to do it for Granny and Jed."

On the same show, "Earl Scruggs" revealed that he had agreed to appear in a commercial for one of banker Drysdale's companies in return for a chance to pitch his own new product.

"For my part, he promised to use my new banjo book on every single commercial," Scruggs said in the episode, during which the book was brandished.

That book, *Earl Scruggs and the Five-String Banjo*, became a huge seller and remains in print and demand, after several revisions, nearly 50 years after its first appearance. It was yet another way for Scruggs to take his work to an increasingly larger audience.

As Flatt and Scruggs consolidated their gains through the 36 annual episodes of *The Beverly Hillbillies*—by February of its third season it matched the 92 total episodes of *Mad Men* between 2007 and 2015—they continued to capture audiences for their own syndicated show. The duo's 30-minute TV offering was often programmed in a block with other syndicated country shows. On WRAL-TV in Raleigh, North Carolina, the lineup was Flatt and Scruggs, the Wilburn Brothers, and Porter Wagoner, from 6 p.m. to 7:30 p.m. Saturday nights. For country and bluegrass fans in fortunate markets, Flatt and Scruggs's Martha White–backed show presented a weekly musical vacation. It was shot and recorded in a straightforward manner, with the music broken up only by intros by Flatt or MC "T. Tommy" Cutrer. The band itself performed many of the commercials, including the popular "Martha White Theme."

This catchy jingle later turned up on the live album that Flatt and Scruggs recorded at Carnegie Hall in 1962. That performance of "Martha White" wasn't planned as part of the show and came only after repeated shouts for it from the audience, creating a humorous backdrop to a memorable performance.

Each syndicated Flatt and Scruggs show virtually guaranteed banjo fans a Scruggs feature such as "Foggy Mountain Breakdown," with his Mastertone front and center in closely framed camera angles. Viewers could learn chords and lyrics by watching Flatt sing as he picked his big 1950 Martin D-28 with his name in a block inlaid on the fingerboard.

In the 21st century, videos of the show are widely available on YouTube or in commercial packages, keeping the 1950s and 1960s Foggy Mountain Boys in demand for a cyber audience. Musicians Jerry Douglas and Béla Fleck both cited Scruggs's picking on the syndicated shows as some of his best work.

Even before *The Beverly Hillbillies* multiplied their fan base, Flatt and Scruggs had been on an upward climb, due in part to the growing folk music boom. They were also enjoying significant hits on country radio according to *Billboard* charts. In 1959 and 1960, they scored *Billboard* successes ranging from the "Cabin on the Hill" at No. 9, "Polka on a Banjo" at No. 12, and "Gone Home" at No. 10. Then came "The Ballad of Jed Clampett," which spent three weeks at No. 1 on the country charts in the show's debut season. "Pearl Pearl Pearl," a novelty based on a plot line in the Beverly Hillbillies, reached No. 8 in May 1963. It featured a rare lead vocal appearance by Scruggs, whose accurate, rich baritone singing enhanced dozens of Flatt and Scruggs recordings.

All this commercial success had another side. Hard-core bluegrass fans tended to find the band's releases in the second half of the '60s less appealing, as their recordings leaned toward novelty and folk songs. In addition, they employed a "stacked" harmony vocal sound using as many as five voices. It fit with the folk sound of the day but didn't suit the ears of those who preferred the Flatt-Seckler duets or the trios with the sky-high vocals of bassist Jake Tullock.

This was especially true among the fans who had found hard-core bluegrass in the 1950s and supported the traditional acts by showing up at personal appearances, taping shows, interviewing and writing about the acts, and, in the case of Ralph Rinzler, even managing Bill Monroe. In the 1950s, a Flatt and Scruggs fan club emerged at Georgia Tech in Atlanta.

In a 2015 interview, the singer, picker, and songwriter Alice Gerrard talked about the way she and friends like Mike Seeger and Rinzler responded to members of the bluegrass pantheon, including Flatt and Scruggs.

"They were fantastic in those days when we were going to see them in the late '50s and early '60s," Gerrard said. "Everybody loved Earl Scruggs. He was like this genius guy."

Gerrard was one of a growing crowd of people, including music scholar Dick Spottswood and *Bluegrass Unlimited* editor Pete Kuykendall, who hadn't necessarily grown up in the tradition but gravitated to bluegrass and old-time music with intense interest and involvement. A native of the West Coast, Gerrard joined West Virginia–born singer Hazel Dickens in a successful duo that lifted people's consciousness about the role of women in bluegrass. Dickens and Gerrard favored the harder-core impact of vocalists such as Ralph Stanley and Bill Monroe to Flatt's singing.

"In some ways, Lester had a slightly more pop sound to his voice. Monroe and the Stanley Brothers, that sound was more akin to what you heard when you listened to Roscoe Holcomb or Dock Boggs or Ola Belle Reed," Gerrard said.

When Mike Seeger, Dickens, Gerrard, and others of the new group of young fans sought out artists to interview, tape, or promote, they typically chose Monroe, the Stanleys, or old-time artists.

"We would go to see them and we would go to see all of those guys," Gerrard said.[10] Rinzler was trying to publicize and promote Monroe as the founder of bluegrass, particularly in light of an article in the popular *Sing Out!* folk music magazine that elevated Scruggs as the central figure of bluegrass. This controversy crystallized in an often cited 1962 exchange between Monroe and Rinzler, who had asked for an interview. "If you want to know about bluegrass music, ask Louise Scruggs," Monroe told Rinzler angrily, referring to Louise's active, successful promotion of Flatt and Scruggs in national media.[11] In the years since, Monroe has occupied such a peak of recognition as the "Father of Bluegrass" that any former neglect by the folk scene seems surprising.

"If you are thinking in terms of who needs the most help here, it's Bill Monroe and the Stanley Brothers," Gerrard said, recalling the era. "Flatt and Scruggs were off doing *The Beverly Hillbillies*." Gerrard and friends, journalists, and documentarians as well as musicians, acted on the principle that whatever promotional assistance they could provide would be better spent on acts whose careers had not shot upward as strongly as Flatt and Scruggs's.

Flatt and Scruggs may have been losing some hipster and critical cachet, but dates and recordings continued to pay off well for them. They were headliners at venues ranging from college campuses to the new hippie halls in California and elsewhere. Audiences of many different backgrounds came out to hear Flatt's amiable MC style and distinctive vocals and Scruggs's powerful banjo.

But in the later '60s, cracks began to appear in the union. The story of their split is widely known, centering on musical differences and an eventual challenge by Flatt to the business arrangements between the two.

It seems, though, that the split also related to changing tastes and manners. Lester Flatt was a down-home person who was glad to stay that way. Wiseman said Flatt would sit with his family on Sunday afternoon before another road trip started. When time came to leave, Flatt would simply get up and walk off, not uttering a word. He was a top-level talent of a different sort, able to convey emotion and humor without apparent effort. Mac Wiseman, a person of considerable girth, remembered getting frequent calls from Flatt in the morning, asking whoever answered the phone, "Is Tiny up yet?"

Scruggs had a more questing intelligence. He enjoyed keeping up with society as it changed. This attention emerged clearly as his three sons, Gary, Randy, and Steve, grew up and came to like different kinds of music. A devoted dad, Earl Scruggs learned about and played with some of their favorite acts, such as Bob Dylan and Joan Baez. (Scruggs had also encountered many folk acts on the performance circuit.)

Dobro man Buck Graves recalled the disruption over the musical direction Scruggs was pushing. This new path frequently found Flatt in the unwelcome position of singing Bob Dylan's abstract, sometimes obtuse words.

"Flatt didn't want to do some of them," Graves recalled. "Some of them was pretty good and some weren't worth a dang far as I was concerned. 'Mr. Tambourine Man,' you know, that, to me, is great stuff right there and we had a good cut on it. But we got a little far out there, and I think it hurt a little bit. Some of it I didn't like to do. I loved Dylan's work, but not all of it."[12]

Even as Flatt and Scruggs drifted apart, another medium—the movies—was to create a space for their last leap upward. It happened in a curious way, when two sharp young magazine writers, Robert Benton and David Newman, put their heads together at locations including Benton's walk-up apartment in New York City. They were crafting what they described as a "French New Wave gangster movie" while listening, over and over, to the original Mercury recording of "Foggy Mountain Breakdown."

The movie became *Bonnie and Clyde*. And the sound of Scruggs's banjo rang out at every step of that movie's path, from the creation of a rough first draft to its appearance in the world's theaters.

12

RIDING WITH
BONNIE AND CLYDE

"Foggy Mountain Breakdown" serves as the "voice" of the breakthrough 1967 film *Bonnie and Clyde* because its star and producer Warren Beatty happened to attend a Virginia high school with the bluegrass picker and record collector Pete Kuykendall.

Or, it's there because Beatty asked Earl Scruggs to write theme music for *Bonnie and Clyde*. Then, like Dorothy about to leave the Land of Oz, Beatty realized that he didn't have to wander through creation to find joy: It was waiting in the backyard. In Beatty's case, the music he wanted lay close at hand in his record collection.

Or, it's there because its two screenwriters sat in *Mad Men*–era apartments and offices in New York City, writing the movie's sad, sardonically violent script while "Foggy Mountain Breakdown," specifically the original Mercury recording, blared over and again in the background.

Each of these versions has a constituency and a story to back it. Whatever the circumstances, "Foggy Mountain Breakdown" became the linchpin of a movie with its own saga, one involving Hollywood moguls and French auteurs, budding acting careers built on nearly nothing, and mighty film critics gone astray and even at war with each other.

"Foggy Mountain Breakdown" posed some controversy when it appeared in *Bonnie and Clyde*: Should banjo music accompany horrific violence? Weren't banjos supposed to be funny?

"At that time when it came out, 'Foggy Mountain Breakdown' was played on commercial radio stations," actor-comedian-banjo player Steve Martin said. "I just thought it was dynamic. I had no idea it was supposed to be funny."[1]

The use of "Foggy Mountain Breakdown" in a movie filled with dark humor and violence provoked different reactions from different quarters because it landed amid the cultural shifts of the '60s. That era has been overly romanticized by many of the 70 million baby boomers who grew up in its midst, but the '60s indeed brought changes in families, relationships, and arts, including music and film.

Bonnie and Clyde and a handful of other films were to transform the prevailing American movie business, where love and violence often appeared bland and punchless. In addition, it toppled America's most powerful movie critic, proving once again that pop celebrity could change as quickly as the Hit Parade.

Creative differences aside, the transitions of the '60s often proved wrenching, as people drew lines between those who embraced a culture viewed as more accepting and free, and those, including "the Greatest Generation," who prided themselves on responsibility and uprightness. That sort of opposition meant that the '60s also saw the team of Lester Flatt and Earl Scruggs reach a parting. Their partnership and the Foggy Mountain Boys name died before the decade ended, 35 years after Bonnie and Clyde's luck ran out.

═══

Bienville Parish, Louisiana, is the spot where the historical Bonnie Parker and Clyde Barrow cleaved to eternity when the armed men they called "laws" drenched them in gunfire. Visitors can explore exhibits at the Bonnie & Clyde Ambush Museum and stop in at Ma Canfield's former café in Gibsland, where the outlaws ate their last breakfast.[2]

However, the historical Bonnie and Clyde shot to bits on the Sailes Road on May 23, 1934, weren't the Bonnie and Clyde seen jerking and dying in the 1967 movie. That scene was filmed at Albertson Ranch in Triunfo, California. Nor were they the same fictional Bonnie and Clyde who had appeared in two previous movie portrayals, or the couple who were to occupy several pop-music treatments. These included Georgie Fame's ragtimey "The Ballad of Bonnie and Clyde," an entire album by Flatt and Scruggs, and the French dance hit "Bonnie & Clyde" by pop stars Serge Gainsbourg and Brigitte Bardot.

In fact, Bonnie Parker and Clyde Barrow were physically small, small-time crooks from Dallas. They emerged murderously as America's first intentional, social-media–style criminals-as-stars. They manufactured publicity, monitoring the press eagerly. They used media, including carefully staged photographs, to promote their string of misdeeds, robbery, and death. Parker wrote poetry and newspapers published her offerings.

Bonnie and Clyde met in January 1930 at a party, but their cross-country criminal episodes didn't rev up immediately. First, Barrow was jailed in Waco for burglary, Parker smuggled him a pistol to aid his escape, and Barrow did more time in Ohio, winning parole in February 1932. Then Bonnie and Clyde got down to business.

According to FBI accounts, Parker and, mostly, Barrow committed the following acts:[3]

- Thirteen murders, committed in towns including Joplin and Columbia, Missouri; Dallas, Abilene, Hillsboro, and Sherman, Texas; and Stringtown and Miami, Oklahoma
- The "liberation" of five prisoners from Eastham State Prison in Waldo, Texas
- Kidnappings of a man and woman in rural Louisiana; a deputy in Carlsbad, New Mexico; a sheriff and the chief of police in Carlsbad, New Mexico; and an attorney whom they abandoned in Miami, Oklahoma
- Attacks on prison guards at Waldo and highway patrolmen in Grapevine, Texas
- "Numerous" bank robberies

They stayed in trouble. They stayed in the news.

Parker's poem "The Story of Bonnie and Clyde" ran in newspapers everywhere as a premature self-obituary, ending:

> Some day they'll go down together;
> And they'll bury them side by side;
> To few it'll be grief
> To the law a relief
> But it's death for Bonnie and Clyde.

The public attention given the Barrow gang came as hillbilly music was peaking in national exposure. The Bristol sessions of 1927 had brought fame to Jimmie Rodgers and the Carter Family, acts who became takeoff points for country music and, eventually, bluegrass. By the time the criminal acts of Bonnie and Clyde were being telegraphed across the country by news media, increasingly powerful AM radio stations such as WBAP in Dallas, WLS in Chicago, and WSM in Nashville could be heard across the nation. In addition to other programming, they broadcast the sounds of banjos and fiddles in hillbilly string bands. The music may have originated on the farms and in the mountain cabins it frequently summoned up, but its commercial form reached many millions of people. It served as a counterpoint to the sophisticated sounds of big-band music and to the citified notions of glamour in film.

A child of the era and region, native Texan Robert Benton wrote the first take of the screenplay of *Bonnie and Clyde* in 1963 along with his *Esquire* magazine colleague David Newman. Born in Waxahatchie in 1932, Benton was shy of two years old when the outlaws Barrow and Parker died in Louisiana. Benton's father, a faithful reader of *True Detective* magazines, attended the separate funerals for the couple who died together but were "buried in different graveyards, miles apart."[4]

Benton grew up hearing their story told and retold during a boyhood spent largely in Dallas. He received a bachelor of fine arts degree in 1953 from the University of Texas at Austin, where his classmates included Jayne Mansfield and Rip Torn. Then Benton headed for New York City but never completed the art history degree he began at Columbia University.[5]

Before long, Benton was working as art director at *Esquire*, the men's magazine then becoming a trendy font of gentlemen's wisdom, featuring luxury goods mixed with New Wave snark. Along with colleague Newman, an *Esquire* editor, Benton produced in 1962 the first rendering of the magazine's Dubious Achievement Awards, a sort of predecessor to the *National Lampoon*, the *Onion*, and Andy Borowitz.

In 2015 interviews, Benton told me that inspiration to write a script for *Bonnie and Clyde* arose both from his childhood recollections and from a passage in John Toland's influential book about John Dillinger and other gangsters, *The Dillinger Days*, which was brand new in 1963. The book captures Parker and Barrow: "They were, in short, not only outlaws, but outcasts."

That would also have been an apt description for characters in *Shoot the Piano Player*, the 1960 film by French New Wave director Jean-Luc Godard. The movie mixed humor and blood by presenting feckless criminals with little expertise. It also located death in a desolate landscape. Benton and Newman were consumed by directors such as Godard and his contemporary François Truffaut, who was to play a key role in the struggle *Bonnie and Clyde* endured just to be born. The screenwriters were completing a circle of sorts, as the French New Wave directors had drawn liberally on violence-ridden American movies such as *Gun Crazy*.

"We decided to write a French movie about a couple of Texas gangsters," Benton told me.

But what of "Foggy Mountain Breakdown"? Wasn't there an early connection between bluegrass music and Warren Beatty, the star and producer of *Bonnie and Clyde*? That tie was detailed by bluegrass chronicler Neil Rosenberg in his definitive work *Bluegrass: A History*.

In a 2014 interview, Pete Kuykendall told me the story of his days in a Virginia high school, where Beatty was also a student. Born March 30, 1937, Beatty encountered Kuykendall at Washington-Lee High School in Arlington in the mid-1950s.

"The only reason I knew Beatty was that we went to high school together," Kuykendall said. "He was kind of a big man on campus."

Beatty was captain of the football team and senior class president. The two notably crossed paths when Kuykendall appeared before Beatty's classroom as part of a career day, when students talked about what they intended to do in later life.

"I wanted to be a DJ," Kuykendall said. "I took three records to school that day: 'Pain in My Heart,' by the Lonesome Pine Fiddlers, and 'Foggy Mountain Breakdown' and another one."

When the class was over, Beatty cornered Kuykendall in the classroom to learn more about the explosive banjo music he had just heard.

"It just had so much fire to it," Kuykendall said. "He kept after me after the class, just quizzing me about what kind of music that was."

When Beatty was involved with choosing the music for *Bonnie and Clyde*, he insisted on the 1949 Mercury version, Kuykendall said. "That one had the fire," he said.

Beatty's love for the original "Foggy Mountain Breakdown" recording also appeared in the story as told by Scruggs.

"Warren Beatty called and wanted me to write a score for the movie," Scruggs said. "And I don't know if I tried anything or what, but anyway, we didn't hear from him for four or five days, and then he called back and said forget writing anything, he had found what he wanted.

"And he found an original 'Foggy Mountain Breakdown,' so he put it in a kind of a loop, where it just keeps going on and on. So that's how that 'Foggy Mountain Breakdown' got in there."

It's possible that all these stories are true, that Beatty first learned about the tune from Kuykendall, coincidentally had it pitched to him by the screenwriters, and asked Scruggs to write a score, before returning to "Foggy Mountain Breakdown."

However, if there's any contradiction, Benton said, his story trumps. "Mine is the Bible," he said.

———

Benton and Newman, taking their first shot at scriptwriting, immodestly picked their hero, Truffaut, whom they did not know, to direct the film. Benton was the Southerner of the pair, but it was Newman, a New Yorker with a deep grounding in music, who brought "Foggy Mountain Breakdown" to the table. "The very first day we sat down to outline the script, David, who had never been to Texas in his life, brought the record over and said, 'This is the music of the picture,'" Benton said. "I thought, 'No way. It's way too early in the process to say this is what the music is.'

"Each step of the way, [Newman] never gave up on 'Foggy Mountain Breakdown.' With Truffaut, he played 'Foggy Mountain Breakdown.'"

And how, in a hotel room setting, did the French auteur greet Scruggs's banjo piece?

"He nodded; it sounded wonderful to him," Benton said.

In the early 1960s, Scruggs and Truffaut were at or near the top of their professions, but in entirely different realms. Folk music and bluegrass had become more broadly popular in the late 1950s and early 1960s, while French art films in the United States remained largely the choice of moviegoers in urban centers and on college campuses.

Bluegrass fans of the day could get heated about the relative merits of Flatt and Scruggs, Bill Monroe, and next-generation acts such as the Osborne Brothers and the Country Gentlemen. But for Benton, Newman, and their illustrious circle of New Yorkers—Benton had broken up with early feminist Gloria Steinem just before working on the script—the French cinema was everything, the core subject of discussion, argument, and pleasure.

"It was a time in New York when most conversations were about movies," Benton said. "Not about painting, not about theater, not about literature, it was about movies. We talked about, 'Who do you like more, Truffaut or Godard?' These were serious discussions. Blood was drawn. The impact of European film was enormous. We began to appraise American film in the light of New Wave criticism."

The saga of how *Bonnie and Clyde* finally found a producer in Beatty and a director in Arthur Penn is long and complicated. It's ably told by Mark Harris in his 2008 volume *Pictures at a Revolution*. I also heard several pieces of the tale from Benton, along with some new lore.

"We wrote this specifically for Truffaut, and we had a couple of readings of *Bonnie and Clyde*. At one of the readings was a woman named Helen Scott, who was a close friend of Truffaut," Benton said.

The treatment got a first rejection from director Arthur Penn but kept making the rounds, reaching Truffaut through Scott. Once he received the treatment, Truffaut was interested enough to have the script translated into French in early 1964. When in New York in March, he met at length with Benton and Newman.

In contrast to Scruggs, who met first-chair musicians mostly after he had developed considerable expertise, these young New York screenwriting novices got a lesson from someone at the top of the profession.

"We met in the Regency Hotel and I think I heard David tell it, at the Algonquin," Benton said. "We spent two days working with him. Whatever lessons we had in screenwriting, Truffaut taught us. We had only written a treatment; it was 80 pages long. It was like a script without the dialogue."

As in the case of many creative projects, time kept passing and possibilities arose and faded. Benton said, "Truffaut said he would love to do it, but he was committed to *Fahrenheit 451*, so he gave it to his good friend Godard."

It was September 1964 when Truffaut turned down the film after an extended courtship. During the same month, Jean-Luc Godard, another top-shelf French director, also came to New York, on the brink of making his futuristic 1966 thriller *Alphaville*. He agreed to direct *Bonnie and Clyde* instead but then left over a balky backer.

"The producer said to Godard, 'This is meant to be shot in the summer'; it was November," Benton said.

"Godard said, 'I'm talking cinema; you're talking meteorology,' and he walked out." This oft-told incident threw *Bonnie and Clyde* off the rails for more than a year. Then, in Paris in 1965, Truffaut, Beatty, and the actress Leslie Caron had a notable meal together.

"Warren, who had gone out with Leslie Caron, was in Paris and met with Truffaut because Warren had a picture he wanted Truffaut to direct and Truffaut didn't want to direct," Benton said.

Perhaps simply to change the subject, Truffaut said no to his request but asked Beatty if he had heard of the wonderful script *Bonnie and Clyde* by two American writers.

Back in New York, Beatty called Benton, who knew him slightly, asking to see the script. Sure, Benton said, they would have it delivered. No, the star said, he would come over right then. To the chagrin of Benton's wife, the handsome Beatty showed at the couple's apartment a few minutes later, before she had had a chance to fix her makeup and do her hair, Benton recalled with amusement.

"We had a meeting with Warren, and we said we would like to get a French director," Benton said. "Warren said, 'No, you've written a French screenplay, you need an American director.' We said, 'The only director we would want would be Arthur Penn.'"

In his mid-20s, Beatty was trying to outgrow an image as a Hollywood playboy too attractive for his own good. He had had notable success with his star turn in the 1961 romance *Splendor in the Grass*, which cast him to type as a high school football captain. He continued acting through a series of less successful films, including the experimental *Mickey One*, with rising star Penn directing. Having failed to entice Truffaut, Beatty launched a successful effort to have Penn reconsider directing *Bonnie and Clyde* and decided on himself as star and producer.

The choice of an actor to play Bonnie Parker was crucial, and the first-line Hollywood names weren't buying. (Flatt and Scruggs's *Beverly Hillbillies* colleague Sharon Tate was among many on the original list.) That brought Faye Dunaway, far from the landmark star she would become, into the mix. After getting a start on Broadway as understudy to emerging feminist actress-director Barbara Loden, Dunaway had been in only two films, *Hurry Sundown* and *The Happening*. Neither won strong reviews or wide audiences.

"Faye wasn't my first choice," Beatty told an interviewer 30 years later.[6] "We'd been turned down by about 10 women. I wanted Natalie (Wood), Jane (Fonda), Tuesday (Weld), Sharon Tate, Ann-Margret. And then I met Faye. I was living in a penthouse suite at the Beverly Wilshire, and I called Arthur, who was downstairs, and I said I'd met an actress I knew he would like.

"I knew Faye was his type. I didn't think she was right for the character. But I told Faye, go down and meet Arthur. Since I've already told him I don't think you're right for the part, I'm sure he'll say he wants you to do the movie. So she went down three floors and he called me and said, 'I want her.'"

Dunaway, slyly sexy and visually striking in a way that contrasted with Beatty's glamour-boy look, created an ideal on-screen chemistry with him. As the small-town waitress willing to die to break the chains of home, she summed up even more explicitly than Beatty the emerging '60s focus on sex, excitement and the rejection of authoritarian boundaries.

═══

To the dismay of studio executives, the shooting of *Bonnie and Clyde* mostly took place in small towns in Texas, with daily work preceded by long discussions about best practices between Beatty, as producer, and Penn. According to Benton in 2015, a hefty portion of the film's success should go to editor DeDe Allen. Her work pointed up the script's slow, uneasy downtimes and glancing relationships among Beatty, Dunaway, and a historically strong supporting cast.

The slow-paced moments in hotel rooms and hideouts gave contrast to the hell-bent-for-leather quickness of the holdups and shootouts. These were often punctuated by "Foggy Mountain Breakdown."

Seen half a century after its making, *Bonnie and Clyde* continues to hit hard. The lead characters appear aimless and lost at times, but intensely driven during the violent scenes of robbery and murder. The fictional Bonnie and Clyde come alive as they take on partners, including Clyde's brother Buck (played by Gene Hackman), his wife, Blanche (Estelle Parsons), and the charismatically dopey sidekick C. W. Moss (Michael J. Pollard).

A performing ensemble as collaborative as a top bluegrass band, they pass among themselves freighted conversation and flashing moments of humor and dread. Key supporting roles are a humiliated lawman (*Andy Griffith Show* staple Denver Pyle) and the fearful, then fond couple played by Gene Wilder and Evans Evans. The shifts in tone create a weirdly compelling flow.

Bonnie and Clyde first enlist the fey mechanic Moss as a confederate and then hook up with Buck and Blanche, with resulting conflict between the couples. A frustrated Bonnie agonizes over Clyde's lack of desire or ability to have sex. She also draws constant disparaging contrasts between the small-town hicks and hillbillies and whatever it is that Bonnie and Clyde are deciding they represent.

Eugene and Velma, the couple played by Wilder and Evans, find themselves surrounded by the Barrow gang, who press their noses against the windows of Eugene's roadster before kidnapping them. The team of criminals turns mainstream citizens into gawked-at freaks. And Sheriff Frank Hamer suffers professional and sexual humiliation by the gang's scheme to shame him in the papers.

As Bonnie and Clyde near their inevitable end, Scruggs's music rolls with the tensions and releases of the story. There's no doubt that "Foggy Mountain Breakdown" elevated *Bonnie and Clyde*, just as the movie lifted the bluegrass staple to status as an internationally recognized pop-culture signature.

It occurred to some bluegrass fans when the movie came out that the three-finger banjo heard in *Bonnie and Clyde* was anachronistic, because the action of the movie takes place long before "Foggy Mountain Breakdown" was recorded. The first music heard in the movie, "Deep in the Arms of Love," a 1929 composition by Lou Davis and Roy Ingraham, fits more closely with the period. Earl Scruggs's banjo wouldn't be heard outside a few Appalachian-region radio stations until 1945, when he went on the Grand Ole Opry with Bill Monroe. However, we remember Scruggs's statement that he had his breakthrough with his own style when he was 10 or 11. He turned 10 on January, 6, 1934. Bonnie and Clyde died a little less than five months later. Though the murderers never heard the results of Scruggs's childhood revelation, this chronology casts a slightly different light on the music's fitness for the era.

Penn had signed the Hollywood composer Charles Strouse to create a score for *Bonnie and Clyde*, and pieces of his work were used, including bluegrass-y interludes played by banjoist Doug and mandolinist Rodney Dillard, with accompanying tenor banjo probably by Los Angeles session regular Tommy Tedesco. But during postproduction, the sound of Scruggs's three-finger banjo kept rising to the top of the mix.

"Without meaning any disrespect to the lovely Charles Strouse score, they kept taking the score down and bringing up 'Foggy Mountain Breakdown,'" screenwriter Benton said. "DeDe Allen used it in the scratch track and it worked."

"Foggy Mountain Breakdown" fades in at 8:21, as the Barrow gang pulls off their first heist, steals a car and heads out of a small town. It's an abbreviated version of about 30 seconds, with clumsy sound editing that repeats one chord sequence and ends with a clipped note. The frenetic music plays as Bonnie climbs all over Clyde in a careening car, unaware that her new partner is "not much of a lover boy."

Additional banjo and fiddle music, not by Scruggs, reappears as the trio's work becomes more intense and is played for higher stakes. Another period tune, "We're in the Money," comes after the tragicomic scene in which Moss's decision to parallel park during a stickup results in Clyde's grotesquely depicted murder of a bank officer.

After the humiliation of Bonnie's forced, extended kiss of Sheriff Hamer, the lawman spits at her, another point when humor and the gang's violent reaction follow close on each other. At 56:32 comes the longest version of "Foggy Mountain Breakdown." It begins with Benny Sims's fiddle solo and is broken up by periodic short comments from survivors and lawmen. Burma Shave signs, dirt roads, and brown pastures form the backdrop as the gang once more makes its getaway to the racing tune.

The banjo accompanies another escape a few minutes later, but it is not bloodless. Buck Barrow is fatally wounded and Blanche is jailed. Bullets, blood, and flames fly everywhere, as Clyde, Bonnie, and Moss barely make their way to Moss's father's house.

There's only one more role for "Foggy Mountain Breakdown," during a sort of false peace the trio finds at the Moss place. Bonnie writes her poem, "The Story of Bonnie and Clyde." Then Clyde gets the idea of sending it to the papers.

"You know what you've done there? You've told my story," Clyde says, before the couple finally consummate their violent partnership.

This time, "Foggy Mountain Breakdown" begins during a cutaway from the sex scene—"You done just perfect," Bonnie reassures Clyde afterward—then Scruggs's Mastertone continues to roll for more than a minute as viewers see a plot to end the couple's lives take shape. The famous jerky cascade of shells and blood, the ambush that ends the story of Bonnie and Clyde, though it lives long in memory, is far shorter than any use of the banjo tune.

Through the mid-1960s and the controversial release of *Bonnie and Clyde*, Flatt and Scruggs had continued to hit high spots, even as the film spent many months navigating uncertain back roads. They made some great music: a tribute to Mother Maybelle and the Carter Family, the live album at Carnegie Hall, a collaboration with Doc Watson, and the influential all-instrumental album *Foggy Mountain Banjo*. There was a first remake of "Foggy Mountain Breakdown," in 1965, which turned off some listeners with its busier sound and nontraditional harmonica by Charlie McCoy.

They stopped appearing as guests on *The Beverly Hillbillies* after the Bonnie and Clyde–themed episode but popped up on the soundtracks of CBS companion pieces, *Petticoat Junction* and *Green Acres*. There was even a plan afoot to cast Scruggs as a railroad conductor on "Petticoat Junction."

All of this show business activity didn't mean that the Foggy Mountain Boys had deserted their customary rounds. They hadn't, in the words of one of their hits, gotten above their raising and still hit the back roads as well as the growing interstate system. On March 10, 1967, Flatt and Scruggs appeared about 11 miles south of Shelby "in person at the Grover School House, Grover, N.C.," according to the *Gaffney Ledger*.[7] Admission was $1.50 for adults and 75 cents for 6- to 11-year-olds.

Less than a month later, on August 4, *Bonnie and Clyde* made its debut at the Montreal Film Festival. When it opened a few days later in New York City, the movie faced a determined enemy in the person of Bosley Crowther, the longtime chief film critic of the *New York Times*. "It puts forth Warren Beatty and Faye Dunaway in the leading roles, and Michael J. Pollard as their sidekick, a simpering, nose-picking rube, as though they were striving mightily to be the Beverly Hillbillies of next year," Crowther wrote in the Times.[8]

Crowther, a highly influential voice who loved big, traditional Hollywood movies such as *Cleopatra*, wrote several more negative pieces about *Bonnie and Clyde*. Such criticisms led Warner Bros. studio to the brink of pulling it from theaters a month or two after its initial release.

"There were people in Hollywood who just hated that movie," Benton said in *Star*, a biography of Beatty. "The thing that ticked Crowther off is that there was banjo music while they were shooting people. It was perceived to be a thumbing-your-nose attitude, a moral flipness, an arrogance, because nobody in this movie ever said, 'I'm sorry I've killed somebody.'"[9]

But *Bonnie and Clyde* also had fans, the same people who would gravitate to leading-edge American films—*The Graduate* and *The Wild Bunch*—as well as European imports such as *Blow-Up* and *The Bride Wore Black*. Pauline Kael, who was to become one of the chief film critics for *The New Yorker*, wrote a long, poetic review of *Bonnie and Clyde* for the magazine's October 27, 1967, issue nearly three months after its debut. Such high-end reviews are more typically timed for the day or week of a picture's release.

"The writers and the director of *Bonnie and Clyde* play upon our attitudes toward the American past by making the hats and guns and holdups look as dated as the two-reel comedy; emphasizing the absurdity with banjo music, they make the period seem even farther away than it is," Kael wrote.[10]

The critics' dueling attitudes about *Bonnie and Clyde* reflected the era's often bitter struggles between disparate outlooks on society and culture. Should America stick with the way people had long accomplished things, as in the way studios made successful movies? Or should the nation turn to an ironic, disruptive, even mocking approach to government, life and culture? As was the case for many Americans, Earl Scruggs lived somewhere in between, steeped in the love of family and traditional ways, while embracing new directions.

Meanwhile, Beatty launched a campaign in his determination to see his movie succeed within this argumentative time. He met Chicago critic Roger Ebert, 25, who had written an early positive review of the film, for an interview in a London hotel room. In explaining to Ebert the movie's sudden shifts of tone, Beatty discussed a scene in which a butcher who is being robbed goes after Clyde with a meat cleaver. Sound mixers quadrupled in volume the sound of Clyde's pistol hitting the side of the butcher's head, Beatty said.

"But then again—we change the sound again," said Beatty, like a high-school quarterback explaining a trick play. "Bonnie and Clyde drive away in their touring car, and on the sound track we have Flatt and Scruggs playing 'Foggy Mountain Breakdown,' giving the whole thing a kind of carnival air. Only this time the music isn't appropriate, see? It's music that says, laugh, but you can't laugh. The whole movie kind of weaves back and forth between making you laugh and making you sick."[11] With enthusiasm and ticket sales growing for the film, Beatty put pressure on the studio to rerelease it, particularly after *Time* magazine featured it on its December 8, 1967, cover.[12]

"*Bonnie and Clyde* is not only the sleeper of the decade but also, to a growing consensus of audiences and critics, the best movie of the year," the magazine said.

Bonnie and Clyde, along with "Foggy Mountain Breakdown," achieved blockbuster status, universally seen and heard, helping to change the fashion for big movies into a taste for films that touched on harder, more controversial themes and on unconventional people. The sound of Flatt and Scruggs's recording, somehow familiar, yet jarring in the movie's context, fit well into a period where old tropes such as gangster films got startling remakes.

Not long afterward, Bosley Crowther lost his job as chief critic at the *New York Times*, a move widely viewed as a reaction to his poor judgment in regard to *Bonnie and Clyde*. An era of moviemaking had begun with *Bonnie and Clyde* and its new Hollywood counterparts, just as bluegrass and exciting banjo music enjoyed a major boost from the popularity of "Foggy Mountain Breakdown."

Earl Scruggs and family had been living in the Nashville suburb of Madison since the mid-1950s. And Gary Scruggs, in his late teens, drove into Music City to see what Beatty and crew had wrought.

"I went to see the movie at a theater in downtown Nashville," he said. "I knew going in that 'Foggy Mountain Breakdown' was somehow used in the film, but I didn't really know what to expect. I came out of the theater that night thinking it was one of the best—if not the best—movies I had ever seen. I was also happily surprised to see that FMB was used more than once during the course of the film."

Gary Scruggs pointed out the deep impact that the soundtrack song had on Flatt and Scruggs: airplay for the 1949 Mercury recording, increased bookings for the act, new recordings that used a "gangster" theme and images, as well as a Grammy award. Widely touted as music's highest honor, a Grammy for best country performance went to Flatt and Scruggs and "Foggy Mountain Breakdown" in March 1969.

"It was the only Grammy ever awarded to Flatt and Scruggs, and it ironically came just a few days after it was announced that Flatt and Scruggs had split up," Gary Scruggs said.

The National Academy of Recording Arts and Sciences, the industry association that presents the Grammys, departed from its usual practice by holding its 1969 Grammy awards presentations in three cities. In addition to events in New York and Los Angeles, the society held a presentation gala at Nashville's National Guard Armory, with Dick Clark as master of ceremonies. Among those accepting awards were Johnny Cash and Zelma Redding, the widow of Memphis-based soul music star Otis Redding.

When the award for "Foggy Mountain Breakdown" was announced, Cash stepped up to receive it.

"Mrs. Scruggs asked me to accept this for Earl," Cash said, according to a *Tennessean* account. "I don't know if Lester is here or not."

Cash hesitated, according to the story, and then said, "I liked 'em both. I wish they'd stick together."[13]

The improbable success of his rapidly written banjo tune was to please and, to some degree, amuse Scruggs throughout his life.

"Years after the film's release, I watched *Bonnie and Clyde* on videotape or DVD at least a couple of times with Dad, and he thoroughly enjoyed it each time," Gary Scruggs said. "And it seemed to me he had a twinkle in his eyes during the chase scenes when 'Foggy Mountain Breakdown' was featured."

Script cowriter David Newman died in 2003. He and Robert Benton had gone on to brilliant careers, winning three Academy Awards between them for writing and directing. Benton has remained proud of *Bonnie and Clyde*, even if the '60s bent for intensity, gaiety, and violence has lost luster.

That '60s mindset, referred to as "the New Sentimentality" in an *Esquire* piece by the screenwriters, emerged in a sort of preface to the script prepared for the meeting with Truffaut, quoted by Harris in *Pictures at a Revolution*.

"If Bonnie and Clyde were here today, they would be hip," the preface said. "Their values have become assimilated in much of our culture—not robbing banks and killing people, of course, but their style, their sexuality, their bravado, their cultivated arrogance, their narcissistic insecurity, their curious ambition have relevance to the way we live now," the note read.

Asked about the note, Benton said in 2015:

"Do I believe that's true? I believe we believed it at the time. They were never meant to be culture heroes. They wanted to be stars. They didn't want to be rich, but they wanted to be celebrities. What they wanted was to be famous."

And if, as Benton has said, "Foggy Mountain Breakdown" is the voice of *Bonnie and Clyde*, what does that voice represent?

"It was an exuberance," he said. "It wasn't melodramatic. Terrible things happened and they did terrible things, but they went against the type. A lot of what people found appealing in the movie, appealing about the characters, was reflected in that particular piece of music."[14]

Moviegoers found something riveting and new in the inventively filmed story of the hapless, doomed criminals, Bonnie and Clyde. Similarly, listeners were captured by the rocketing energy of "Foggy Mountain Breakdown" despite its difference from virtually anything else on the late-1960s pop-music scene.

13

SCRUGGS WITHOUT FLATT
A PERIOD OF TRANSITION

Throughout the 1960s, Flatt and Scruggs worked a well-established professional circuit of college campuses, television studios, recording sessions, nightclubs, concert halls, and the occasional schoolhouse. As the act approached its final years, Flatt and Scruggs made several high-impact appearances.

Early in 1969, Flatt and Scruggs were chosen to represent Tennessee on the state's parade float for the inauguration of President Richard M. Nixon. The Foggy Mountain Boys rode the float on January 20, 1969, but the crowd heard a recorded version of "Foggy Mountain Breakdown" played over a sound system. The Oxon Hill Cloggers, from a nearby Maryland community, danced on the float as the tableau moved along the route.[1]

But even "Foggy Mountain Breakdown" couldn't save Nixon, though the young California comedian Steve Martin, already playing bluegrass banjo in his act, suggested it might have, after the President resigned in 1974:

"As part of a bit about the banjo being such a happy instrument. . . . I always thought the banjo was the one thing that could have saved Nixon. . . . He gets off the plane, says, 'I'd like to talk about politics, but first, a little "Foggy Mountain Breakdown"'."[2]

As late as February 16, 1969, Flatt and Scruggs continued to hit the small-town venues that had paid their bills for so many years. That day, a Sunday, they were billed for shows at 2:30 p.m. ($3) and 8 p.m. ($3.50) at the Meadville, Pennsylvania, High School Auditorium.[3] The final Flatt and Scruggs live performance was on the Grand Ole Opry at the Ryman Auditorium in Nashville on February 22, 1969.

In March 1969, the month of Grammy recognition, Cohen Williams, their champion for many years at Martha White Flour, let the press know that the duo would soon pick no more. "I tried to hold them together as a team, but it looks like they are splitting," Williams told the Associated Press.

They broke up the partnership amid bitter words, lawsuits, and recrimination. Then they reconciled their differences, legally at least, before setting off alone as leaders of separate bands.

Flatt was angry and puzzled over the split. Suspicious by nature, he took his partner to court, suing Earl and Louise Scruggs in April while alleging "embarrassing behavior" on Earl's part and fraud by Louise.[4] They countersued. Before 1969 was over, an audit was completed and the disputed matters were resolved. And the lawyers managed to put a good face on the dispute as the settlement was announced.

"The original conflict had arisen out of a lack of communications, and when all the facts had been revealed, through all parties of interest, it was found that there was no real basis for disagreement between them," attorneys Grant Smith, representing Flatt, and Harlan Dodson, for Scruggs, said in a December 1 statement. "Accordingly, they dissolved their partnership interests on a friendly basis."[5]

One of the casualties of the settlement was the name "Foggy Mountain Boys," which both partners agreed not to use. The duo who had created so much great music and crossed so many creeks and cultural boundaries would never play together again. During the courtroom wrangling, the newspapers noted, Flatt and Scruggs didn't speak to each other.

Flatt and Scruggs fell mostly on opposite sides of the classic '60s-era disputes—Flatt with his traditionalism and dislike of hippies, drugs, and long hair, and Scruggs with his adventurous musicality, openness to change, and occasional political activism. They also had a lot in common. Scruggs had his own deeply traditional values of home and family and always rooted his playing in whatever style of music—in the values of tone, timing, and taste—he had honed from boyhood. Despite his grouchiness about change, Flatt had, for decades, showed his ability to adapt to different kinds of people and places. He built rapport with New York audiences and with counterculture crowds in the concert venues of the West Coast. His singing remained strong and vibrant, if sometimes unenthusiastic on the newer material the Foggy Mountain Boys recorded.

"During the last months Earl and I were together, there was constant pressure to modify our sound to give it a bit of rock flair," Flatt told Canadian interviewer Ron Clingen not long after the breakup.[6]

As Gary Scruggs recalled, Flatt and Scruggs had developed a following beyond bluegrass circuits several years earlier. These ventures laid the groundwork for the act that would become the Earl Scruggs Revue.

"My brother Randy and I sat in with Flatt and Scruggs when they appeared at the huge Miami Pop Festival in December of 1968," Gary said in an email. "It was a multi-genre music festival with many acts, including the Grateful Dead, Steppenwolf, Procol Harum, Joni Mitchell, José Feliciano, and Marvin Gaye.

"F&S was the only country act on the bill, and I believe it's quite possible they were invited to perform largely because of the popularity of 'Foggy Mountain Breakdown' being used in the film *Bonnie and Clyde*. F&S was received well by the audience, and I remember the biggest response during the set was following 'Foggy Mountain Breakdown.'"

Scruggs was decisive about the direction he wanted to pursue and about making music with his sons. Flatt was suspicious about the way the act's money was being split up and adamant about his dislike of the modernistic sound. There appeared to be no room for compromise.

Years later, Josh Graves said that Flatt was bitter about the split for many years. Flatt had been content with the tradition-oriented side of the band, as witnessed by his performance after the breakup of much of the former repertoire.

"I'm sure it was like a new adventure to him," Graves said. "To me, it would be like losing your arm, after Earl had been standing next to him for so long."[7]

As a point of cultural reference, another signature '60s act, the Beatles, also headed for a split around the same time. Within the same month that Flatt and Scruggs played the inaugural parade, the Beatles gave their last public performance, at the rooftop concert on January 30, 1969.

John Lennon and Paul McCartney had met at the church-sponsored gathering known as Woolton Fete on July 6, 1957. The friends formed a succession of bands, topped the pop world as the Beatles, and announced their breakup in April 1970. Making roughly similar climbs from obscurity to the top of their fields, both groups lived through the same fraying and breakup over musical and personal conflicts.

"Nothing gold can stay," Robert Frost wrote about the peak of nature's perfection. In musical partnerships, it seems, the intensity and creativity that builds bonds can ultimately pull them apart.

The 24 years Earl Scruggs had spent at the side of Lester Flatt had created a legacy with few parallels in American music. From endless road dates with Bill Monroe to television stardom and Hollywood exposure, the team had become the most commercially successful bluegrass act. They would retain that status until Alison Krauss came along decades later and sold millions of records with a bluegrass-indie-folk mix.

With the partnership dissolved, Earl Scruggs showed no sign of slowing his pace or his love for picking. For all the success he had enjoyed with Flatt, he was ready for something new. "I just got tired of playing 'Cripple Creek' and 'Cumberland Gap' over and over and over again," Scruggs said later. "I had gone about as far as I could with the banjo in bluegrass music."[8]

In those days, the national publication *Family Weekly* had a feature called "Ask Them Yourself" that let readers put questions to famous people. In 1971, Henry Ross of Lansing, Michigan, wanted to know why Flatt and Scruggs broke up.

"The press made our parting sound a lot less friendly than it really was," came Scruggs's answer. "Lester wanted to return to the original way we had done music in 1948, while I was more interested in modern things. Learning a new tune has always been exciting for me. And then I had been on the road for almost 20 years. I wanted to be with my children."[9]

≡≡≡

As early as 1960, a collaboration with R&B sax man King Curtis had showed Scruggs some new directions the banjo could take. "That session really turned me on to playing different types of music," Scruggs said. "It was really the turning point with my music."[10]

Scruggs's account of his playing "Foggy Mountain Breakdown" with King Curtis indicated that it took place between tapings of other performances on *Folksound USA*. No recording of the jam seems to exists, and Curtis is not listed as a performer. However, a tape of the *Folksound* show, viewable only at the Paley Center archives in New York City, shows the blues singer Mildred Anderson accompanied by a saxophonist seen only in shadow, who looks and sounds like Curtis. It would have been wonderful to hear what the two distinctive talents produced.

"I'd never played with a good horn player before," Scruggs recalled. "I'm always listening for a new sound, so I agreed. I was surprised how well the banjo worked with a saxophone, and that got my attention really fast. I realized the banjo could work in a lot of different situations."[11]

The Scruggs collaboration wasn't the first cross-genre jam Curtis had joined. On September 10, 1958, he and rock 'n' roll immortal Buddy Holly had recorded alongside a young Waylon Jennings in an improbable rendition of Harry Choates's Cajun classic "Jole Blon." Holly biographer John Goldrosen wrote that the musicians had tried in vain to translate Choates's Cajun French into English.

A couple of years after jamming with Scruggs, Curtis recorded an all-country disc called *Country Soul* with sax-led renditions of country & western standards and even of such venerable tunes as the Sons of the Pioneers' "Tumblin' Tumbleweeds."

Scruggs's encounter with Curtis and playing with sons Randy and Gary led him to thinking about ways in which the five-string could fit with rock 'n' roll and blues, and the way bluegrass might sound with more aggressive instrumentation and rhythm sections.

Curtis's eagerness to work with Scruggs in 1960 was one of the first indications that players from other genres would flock to work with the banjo virtuoso. And Scruggs's willingness to reciprocate meant that his banjo style would continue to expand the audiences for country and bluegrass.

With striking insight, New York University literary and cultural critic Perry Meisel picked up on country music's influence on King Curtis in his 1998 book, *The Cowboy and the Dandy*. As Curtis developed his own style, Meisel wrote, he wanted to avoid the post-bebop direction of John

Coltrane, with his towering, angular peals of notes that explored radically new harmonies.

"The direction is the style of the banjo, fiddle, and picking guitar—bluegrass styles adapted to horn usage," Meisel wrote, noting that black musicians had made frequent use of fiddle and banjo before the Civil War.

In the same piece, Meisel might have been describing Scruggs's banjo style when he wrote, "The country mode also allows Curtis to push the horn beyond [Louis] Jordan's and [Earl] Bostic's example, too, into a simpler, sharper, and more pointed percussive relation to a rocking rhythm section."

Reached by email in 2016, Meisel said he had never heard of the Scruggs-Curtis meeting, but that it "made perfect sense."[12] He said that his thoughts about Curtis's country influence had been derived from some knowledge of the saxophone player's Texas boyhood and from careful listening.

"It's nice when history confirms after the fact what was originally simply a critical insight," Meisel said.

———

The King Curtis–Earl Scruggs connection is worth pondering on several levels. It brought forward the African American origins of the banjo and the way they influenced both Scruggs and Curtis. And it foreshadowed the myriad mixtures of roots music, jazz, and world music that would enliven offerings for listeners of several generations.

In 2016, singer and banjo player Rhiannon Giddens won the Steve Martin Prize for Excellence in Banjo and Bluegrass, a distinction that had previously gone only to white males. Giddens, who refers to herself as a person of mixed race,[13] has not performed bluegrass per se, but her renditions of black string-band music, along with a multitude of other styles, completed a circle of sorts. In another connection across racial lines, Ann Miller Woodford, a historian of the African American legacy in Western North Carolina, told me in 2018 that her family listened to Flatt and Scruggs and other country musicians "all the time" via broadcasts.

"It was on our black and white TV," said Woodford, 71 when interviewed. "We'd sing along with them. It was one of our favorite times of the day." Especially in gospel music, she said, it was easy to pick out the black church's influence on country and bluegrass music.

Despite decades of almost exclusively white performance, bluegrass has contained African American elements since its founding. That sound comes out in the bends, slides, and syncopation of Scruggs-style banjo, as well as in gospel singing and bluesy elements heard in Bill Monroe, the Stanley Brothers, and their many followers.

≡≡≡

Earl Scruggs started letting his broader musical influences show. Rock 'n' roll and blues loomed larger as Scruggs set off with sons Gary and Randy and a shifting cast of side musicians. They became a top touring attraction in the 1970s, playing before crowds who liked the bluegrass in the show and the rock-based excursions, too.

Back home in the Nashville suburbs, businesslike Louise Scruggs was corresponding with folklorist Archie Green, a major Flatt and Scruggs fan at the University of Illinois, where he was on the faculty and advised a folklore club. The letters offer hints of the new direction Scruggs was taking with the help of his sons and assorted companions. Their debut as the Earl Scruggs Revue came in spring of 1969, with California musicians joining Scruggs and sons in performance.

"Earl made his first appearance in Gatlinburg, Tennessee, a week ago last Saturday at a folk festival," Louise Scruggs wrote Archie Green on June 6, 1969. The May 24, 1969, performance was at the Smoky Mountain Folk Festival.

"The group went over great, and we were extremely happy with the reception," Louise Scruggs wrote. "We have a couple of boys from the West Coast, and they can really get their teeth into the folk songs. They opened the show with 'Down on Penny's Farm,' and did 'Peg and Awl,' 'Dark as a Dungeon' and Gary sang 'Pretty Boy Floyd.' Randy has become quite good with the guitar and the banjo, and they just about brought the house down."

The West Coast musicians were Travis Murphy and Boomer Castleman, who had worked with Michael Martin Murphey, Michael Nesmith, and others. Some early Earl Scruggs Revue appearances featured session guitarist Charlie Daniels, the future Southern rock star, as the only musician outside the Scruggs family.

During the same week, Flatt was also back on the road, playing a show headlined by country star Sonny James at the Capitol Theatre in Ottawa,

Canada. The prohibition against either partner's use of the Foggy Mountain Boys name had not taken effect. And Flatt certainly wasn't about to part ways with the huge audience response he could count on from "Foggy Mountain Breakdown."

"Lester Flatt—with Foggy Mountain Boy Vic Jordan doing his best to turn in some of the five-string banjo work that made Earl Scruggs famous before the pair split—made it clear bluegrass music is far from dead," reviewer Ron Clingen wrote. "The old Capitol Theatre came alive to the down to earth picking and singing of 'Wabash Cannonball,' 'Foggy Mountain Breakdown' from *Bonnie and Clyde*, 'Rollin' in my Sweet Baby's Arms' and many more."[14]

Neither Flatt nor Scruggs would slow the pace of performance or recordings for years to come. And Scruggs entered an arena where only a handful of country artists would go: national and international politics. On November 15, 1969, Scruggs, his older sons, and Daniels played "Foggy Mountain Breakdown" at a mass rally in Washington, D.C., called the Moratorium to End the War in Vietnam. In footage of the rally, the crowds seem to respond as strongly to the tune as followers at the Opry or a bluegrass festival. Family members said later that Scruggs had long opposed the war. Being free to speak up about it seemed to be another opportunity opened to him by his split with Flatt.

"I think the people in the South are just as concerned as the people that's walking the streets here today," Scruggs said in a filmed interview after his performance before hundreds of thousands of protesters. "I'm sincere about bringing our boys back home. I'm disgusted and in sorrow about the boys we've lost over there. And if I could see a good reason to continue, I wouldn't be here today."[15]

This occasion alone, not quite twenty years after the initial recording of "Foggy Mountain Breakdown," showed how far the player and tune had traveled. From an instrumental committed to tape by a relatively obscure country band, "Foggy Mountain Breakdown" had become a piece so widely known that it brought cheers from a huge gathering of the counterculture.

≡

Scruggs kept up with a lot of people—famous musicians and some relative novices. In those days, pop stars such as Bob Dylan, Joan Baez, and the Byrds kept up shields of privacy and seemingly deliberate obscurity.

Yet Dylan, a primary figure in the evolution of pop, shows up on *Earl Scruggs: The Bluegrass Legend—Family & Friends*, a documentary filmed during several years in the late '60s and early '70s. The show also featured Baez, the Byrds, and electronic music pioneer Gil Trythall, who offered up an early synthesizer version of "Foggy Mountain Breakdown." The documentary, which has appeared under a variety of names, was one of the first films made by the influential West Coast documentarian David Hoffman.

Dylan's scene was shot in the Carmel, New York, home of the Flatt and Scruggs album-cover illustrator Thomas B. Allen.[16] Filmmaker Hoffman shows Dylan and Scruggs in December 1970, joined by Randy and Gary on guitar and bass. Dylan, in his bearded *New Morning* look, sings the old-time and bluegrass standard "East Virginia Blues." He and Scruggs even exchange smiles during the taping. Then they roll through a version of Dylan's instrumental "Nashville Skyline Rag," which Scruggs recorded and often performed.

Also for the documentary, the Byrds came to a farm owned by the family of Nashville journalist Doug Underwood. They were filmed recording another Dylan tune, "You Ain't Going Nowhere," with Earl, Randy, and Gary Scruggs. Doug Underwood's daughter, the journalist Paula Underwood Winters, recalled the scene in 2015.[17]

"When my dad told me that Earl was going to shoot part of his PBS special *Earl Scruggs, His Family and Friends* at our farm, I was excited," Winters wrote. "Then I found out The Byrds were going to be there too and that was really exciting. . . .

"We had two log cabins out in our backyard and that's where they set up all the instruments for the shoot. Not wanting to be in the way, but wanting to watch all the action, I climbed up on our roof where I could watch everything but stay out of the camera shots. I had a 'byrd's' eye view!

"I remember a car full of young 'ladies' driving up, and I asked who they were. Someone said they were groupies, and that was my first introduction to what a groupie was. But they stayed out of the way, and I didn't really talk to them. The 15-year-old me was much too shy. . . .

"My mom loves to tell about walking into the bathroom after some of them left and it smelling funny. She said something to Earl's wife, Louise, and Louise told her it was probably marijuana. Mom had no idea what that was.

"I still love watching the Byrds segment on YouTube and wishing I could go back to that time and ask all the questions I have now all these years later."

Despite her efforts to hide, Winters and a friend are visible in some shots, peeking from the cabin roof as the Byrds, including the renowned bluegrass guitarist Clarence White, play country rock with Earl Scruggs in the hills outside Nashville.

<hr />

But Scruggs went far beyond established stars when asked to tell his story for the documentary. With film crew in tow, he returned to Cleveland County to reunite with the Morris Brothers, his earliest professional bosses. Wiley and Zeke had seemed like such music-business pros when Grady Wilkie drove a young Scruggs to South Carolina for a tryout. The Morrises are distinguishable in the footage because their shirts display sewn nametags, part of their work clothes for the car-repair business that for years had earned them a living.

"They tear 'em up and we fix 'em," Wiley says, smiling. "Back when we was in music years, it was come easy, go easy, and God sent Sunday every day."

Scruggs gets out his banjo and all, including some unidentified women in the background, play and sing "On Top of Old Smoky," the brothers' most requested number. It's a moment of inexpressible sweetness, as Scruggs connects with his career before Monroe, before Flatt, and certainly before radio, television, and movies transformed his life.

"Going back to old Smoky, old Smoky so high, where the wild birds and the turtle doves, they can hear my sad cry," the brothers sing.

<hr />

In 1971, Scruggs became a key participant in *Will the Circle Be Unbroken*, a 1972 double album on which the West Coast folk-pop act the Nitty Gritty Dirt Band played with some of the great names of traditional music, including Doc Watson, Roy Acuff, Maybelle Carter, Jimmy Martin, and Merle Travis. Ever his own man, Bill Monroe could not be enticed to join the *Circle* crew, who irked some hard-core fans by adding harmonica and drums to bluegrass arrangements.

"Earl Scruggs called Bill several times trying to get him to be a part of it," former Blue Grass Boy Doug Hutchens wrote in a 2014 Facebook post. "I answered the phone at least four times. Bill said, 'No, we have about a week of dates up in Canada.'"

The record went on to become a bestseller that notably broadened the audience for acoustic music and has since been twice reprised by the act. A 21st-century rerelease of *Circle* included a previously unreleased version of "Foggy Mountain Breakdown," an outtake from the 1972 set. Overall, Earl and sons, particularly Randy, were key to the conception and execution of the Circle records, another example of the Scruggs family's broad impact and drive to keep moving in music.

Similarly, the Earl Scruggs Revue built a new image for Earl and a big audience through constant touring and appearances on popular television shows such as *Austin City Limits* and *The Midnight Special*. Scruggs continued to attract collaborators of the highest caliber. On February 19, 1975, Johnny Cash recorded a spoken introduction to his rendition of "I Still Miss Someone" on a Revue disc released in 1976.[18]

"When I started out in the music business in 1955, I'd long been a fan of Earl Scruggs and his style of banjo picking," Cash said on the recording. "And one of my big thrills, a big highlight of my life, was when I got to work some show dates with him in 1957 and we spent a lot of time backstage in the dressing room just picking and singing what we felt.

"We liked to play around with my songs sometimes and try out his sound on some of my songs. That was another big kick to me, hearing Earl Scruggs play banjo on some of my songs."

The rocked-out side of the Revue was not to everyone's taste. Hard-core bluegrass fans complained about the kinds of songs selected, the presence of electric overload and the placement of Scruggs in situations where they thought the banjo simply didn't fit.

"Earl Scruggs in the context of Lester Flatt and the band, he was perfect," Alan Munde said. "Earl thought his music fit in all kinds of music. My feeling is that it doesn't. When I hear Earl outside the context of Lester Flatt, it's not as attractive."

Munde's opinion echoed the words of the fans who had also had problems with the increasingly modern sound of Flatt and Scruggs in the later 1960s. Purists loved the sound of Flatt's singing and the songs he favored, as well as the mostly straight-ahead bluegrass picking Scruggs offered from 1948 to the mid-1960s. This was the same group of listeners who criticized such central figures as J. D. Crowe and the Osborne Brothers for using electric bass and drums to keep up with the times. The Earl Scruggs Revue never pretended to be a bluegrass band and rarely hit the festival circuit, instead touring colleges and concert halls for a decade. In its day, the Revue found armies of fans who liked the electrified sound linked to five-string rolls. The Revue became a major college-campus attraction during the 1970s, and Earl was able to achieve his dream of working with his boys.

("The Earl Scruggs Revue taught me everything I needed to know about music in the '70s," singer-songwriter Rosanne Cash was to say at a sad occasion, the 2018 memorial service for Randy Scruggs. Very often at Earl's side, Randy honored his father's musical legacy while making his own name as a stellar picker, performer, songwriter, and record producer. He died April 17, 2018, leaving brother Gary to note at the memorial that he was the lone remaining member of his family.)

Managing the Revue, Louise Scruggs continued to make a name for herself as one of the savviest management minds in the business. Musicians such as Foggy Mountain Boy Josh Graves and the fiddler Vassar Clements spent years with the Revue, revving up the musical values and keeping alive Scrugg's connection with mainstream bluegrass.

═══════

While Scruggs was experimenting with new music, large groups of fans were heading backward in time: to 1945, when Scruggs joined Monroe; to 1949, when "Foggy Mountain Breakdown" was committed to tape; and to 1952, when Scruggs developed tuners that enabled the swoops and bends heard in tunes such as "Flint Hill Special," "Randy Lynn Rag" and "Earl's Breakdown."

These fans, especially the banjo players, came to the opinion that no matter how well the Revue did, no matter how many records the *Circle* sold to country and rock fans, there was nothing like the sound of first-generation bluegrass, especially when played on a prewar, flathead Gibson Mastertone.

In September 1971, a baker's dozen of banjo players showed up at the Camp Springs, North Carolina, festival to play a marathon version of "Foggy Mountain Breakdown" in Scruggs's honor. Just before the tune started, the typically taciturn Scruggs took the mic to express how he felt about tackling the tune with top players such as J. D. Crowe, Alan Munde, Sonny Osborne, Randy Scruggs, Bill Emerson, and others.

"That really fills my heart with joy," Scruggs said. "I'm picking with some guys that play a tremendous amount of banjo." Then he shook hands with Osborne and kicked off "Foggy Mountain Breakdown."

Then 24, Munde recalled the day vividly during a 2015 interview.[19] He was playing in the band of another leading bluegrass figure, former Blue Grass Boy Jimmy Martin, and had already recorded the first-generation newgrass disc *Poor Richard's Almanac* with a teenaged Sam Bush. Yet Munde felt lost in the presence of Earl Scruggs. He remembered seeing Scruggs before the banjo fest in what passed for a dressing room at Camp Springs, observing that Scruggs's hands looked shaky.

"But when we were up on stage, he played 'Foggy Mountain Breakdown,' and as soon as he just made a sound on the banjo, it sounded really good to me," Munde said. "I just thought, 'I should not be here.' I would have been really happy just to listen.

"In the end I was glad I was there, and I'm glad I did it."

The show was filmed as part of a movie called *Bluegrass Country Soul*, and, in footage available on YouTube, viewers can see the delight of first-rank players such as Osborne and Crowe simply to be on the stage making music with Scruggs.

Generations of banjoists, including Roni Stoneman, Mike Munford, Kristin Scott Benson, Jim Mills, and Béla Fleck, had their individual moments of revelation upon hearing Scruggs for the first time. Then, like dreamers determined to count drops of rain, they dedicated themselves to unraveling the roll and learning its many variations, as well as spending years searching for the perfect banjo. Most concluded that no matter how excellent they became as players, they would never quite achieve the sound, the grace, the balance, and the beauty that was the three-finger Scruggs style as played by Scruggs. After learning all they could from Scruggs, they developed their own styles based on his foundation. And their numbers grew and their expertise increased, even as the Flatt and Scruggs years receded into the past.

═══

As Scruggs went on his way, Flatt kept on working. He maintained the core of the Foggy Mountain Boys, at least at first. Top-ranked players such as Roland White, Vic Jordan, reliable Curly Seckler, and a teen-aged Marty Stuart also played with Flatt. He made solo records for RCA Victor and other labels after his contract with Columbia lapsed. Drawing on old connections, he recorded and performed with stars such as Mac Wiseman and, of all people, Bill Monroe. Flatt kept "Foggy Mountain Breakdown" in the set list as long as he worked. But for whatever reason, Scruggs drew larger crowds, got soundtrack gigs such as one for the 1974 movie *Where the Lilies Bloom*, and built a large, unshakable following for his music.

In the end, no one could really sing like Flatt, or get across to a crowd the way he did. Just as there will never be another Earl, there will never be another Lester.

Flatt was sick for several months in 1978 and got a visit from Scruggs that was inspired by Flatt's one-time artistic nemesis Bob Dylan. Marty Stuart has told the story that Dylan heard that Scruggs and an ailing Flatt weren't speaking. Dylan told Stuart that he hoped that they would, to avoid a situation like that of feuding film duo Abbott and Costello, who stayed at odds until it was too late. Flatt died at 64 on May 11, 1979, but not before Scruggs visited him at Nashville's Baptist Hospital. He and Flatt talked for about an hour. Apparently, the idea arose that they might play again, although Scruggs told Flatt that he should be thinking more about recovering his health than about working.

Flatt's manager, Lance LeRoy, discussed that last meeting with me in 1999 as I was preparing the notes to a Bear Family Records boxed set, *Flatt on Victor*. In words that also appear in that set, Leroy said that Scruggs visited when Flatt was on his deathbed.[20]

"Deep down Lester never lost his respect for Earl in the slightest," LeRoy said. "He loved Earl. He said, 'Earl don't speak to me and I don't speak to him, but that SOB, nobody could touch him.'

"Tears ran down his cheeks. He couldn't speak above a whisper, but he was the happiest man in the world to see Earl come in and sit."

14

SCRUGGS'S BANJO GAINS A CULT FOLLOWING

Each year in the depths of winter, more than 250 people gather in the East Tennessee hills to admire and pick some of the finest bluegrass banjos in the world. The get-together, called Banjothon, has taken place in a Knoxville hotel in recent years. Earlier incarnations met in living rooms and senior centers. Banjothon unites people who have put untold time, devotion, and, quite often, money into certain rare types of vintage Gibson banjos. They love Earl Scruggs and can sit for hours playing Scruggs numbers that they've played thousands of times before.

Farther east, in North Carolina, a smaller group has signed up twice a year for seminars at the home of player and collector Jim Mills. For roughly the price of a ticket to a reunion of a famous heavy metal band, a banjo enthusiast could spend all day absorbing the lore of the finest bluegrass banjos and hearing Scruggs-style picking from an expert.

Meanwhile, in the international world of commerce, there are stores—at least two of them in Nashville—where people know, discuss, respect, work on, buy and sell a certain kind of banjo: The prewar flathead Mastertone, a banjo closely associated with Earl Scruggs. (The term *flathead* refers to the configuration of the banjo's drumlike head. We'll get back to it and other terms of art.)

These activities center on banjos made in the years before World War II by the Gibson musical instrument company of Kalamazoo, Michigan. The Gibson firm, originally known for its mandolins and guitars, developed an extensive banjo line in the 1920s and into the 1930s. Some of their instruments grew ever more ornate and complicated in response to the demand for Jazz Age music and glitz. Most of these were four-string tenor or plectrum models, designed for pop and jazz music, to be played with a flat pick.

However, the most desirable for today's collectors is the original five-string flathead Granada model with one-piece flange (a connective piece), a gold-plated Gibson made in the late 1920s and into the 1930s. The Granada was fancy but not the company's highest-end banjo.

The flathead Granada made with a short fifth string, called the RB-Granada for "regular banjo," cost $200 according to the 1930–1931 catalog. That's about $3,000 in today's dollars.

The five-string banjo owes its short string to its African ancestor known as the akonting, among many other names. The five-string's principal uses when the greatest Mastertones were made were not only for some Southern string music but also for the "classic" banjo repertoire, in which players followed written music to play rags, cakewalks, and other favorites of the day. In its 1930–1931 catalog, Gibson made a pitch for the five-string's musical viability: "There is every indication that the future of this instrument will be a glorious one and that those who equip themselves to stand out as accomplished artists with the five-string banjo will profit accordingly." A photo of Scruggs's future Grand Ole Opry colleague Uncle Dave Macon equipped with a Gibson five-string illustrates the page of the Gibson catalog facing that prediction.[1]

━━━

Earl Scruggs and his playing style propelled the banjo as an instrument and acoustic string band music as a style from the 1940s into the present era. Similarly, his choice of a 1930 Gibson Granada flathead has meant that vintage flathead Mastertones have become objects of study, preservation, and ongoing commercial appeal.

"For sure, Earl Scruggs is responsible in my opinion for us sitting here," Mills said at his Pre-War Gibson Seminar in his banjo showroom not far from Raleigh. "There's a lot of parallels between these banjos and with violins from the 1700s. They have not improved the design of the violin in

300 years. And they have not improved the design of the banjo since the 1930s."

An all-original flathead RB-Granada from 1930, in as-new condition, sold in late 2015 for $385,000. Known as the "Scotland Granada," the banjo went for roughly the then-current price of a two-bedroom, two-and-a-half-bathroom house in the fashionable Green Hills neighborhood of Nashville.

Why are these banjos worth so much? "It's hands-down the best banjo, and not only that, they haven't figured out how to make them again," said Béla Fleck, who plays a 1937 style 75 flathead Gibson.

Also, they're rare. Only 17 Granadas Mastertones, according to factory records, were made before World War II with the most desirable configuration: 5-string neck, high-profile flathead tone ring, and one-piece flange. Many vintage instruments are rare without being particularly desirable to bluegrass players and collectors. Most people in this area of obsession, if asked why this particular type of banjo commands so much respect, would offer some variation of Mills's response: "Earl played one." And he played one because it had the sound and the tone he required for the music he wanted to play.

"He was without a doubt the singular force in the revival of the five-string banjo after World War II," Johnny Baier of the American Banjo Museum said of Scruggs at Banjothon in 2014. "He wasn't the only force, but it all came together with him."

―――

Scruggs played his Granada from 1949, when he traded Don Reno for it, until his death in 2012. It presented his voice on most of the great Flatt and Scruggs recordings, as well as those of the Earl Scruggs Revue and the all-star recordings he made later in his career. Its sound on "Foggy Mountain Breakdown" perfectly showed off its punch, its voice, its call to the wild.

"In the end, what Earl did, he made the banjo *sound* better," Alan Munde said. "In 'Foggy Mountain Breakdown,' the opening theme is pretty much open-string sorts of things, so there's nothing there to diminish the sound of the banjo. Earl just was full-throated. To play 'Foggy Mountain Breakdown' without that tone is not very interesting."[2]

Scruggs's banjo, an RB-Granada with the factory order number #9584-3, has distinct articulation, balance from its highest to lowest notes, and a fullness and warmth that keep its sound from turning harsh.

Because of their quality, rarity, and connection to Earl, these specific Granadas bring the highest prices.

"In the world of pre-war Gibson banjos, there is no model more legendary than the original five-string Granada with one-piece flange and flathead tone ring," Atlanta banjo player and expert Greg Earnest said. "Fewer than 20 of these banjos were produced, making them many times rarer than Martin's famed pre-war D-45 guitars."[3]

Virtually every aspect of the Granada is crucial to its sound and value, according to players and collectors. And banjos have many variables, making them inherently more complicated than guitars or mandolins.

"All-original" is a term of highest praise for Mastertone aficionados. These collectible banjos have numerous parts, large and small. Owners can switch and replace a few key parts, for a variety of reasons. Sometimes, the changes occur to the detriment of the banjo's value and sound.

"Bluegrass banjoists are especially fond of the mechanical quality of their instruments; the nuts and brackets, flanges, tailpiece and bridge invite constant mechanical adjustment," Karen Linn, an archivist at the Library of Congress, wrote in *The Half-Barbaric Twang: The Banjo in American Popular Culture*.

"Because of the modernizing innovations of banjo manufacturers at the end of the 19th century and during the 1920s," Linn explained, "the banjo is a machine, inviting manipulation."

It's said that banjos are like vintage automobiles in some respects. Originality is valued in both, but just as car collectors can replace carburetors and tie rods, banjo owners can replace everything from tuners to tailpiece.

"A banjo's 50 percent nuts and bolts, so they lend themselves to hotrodding, switching out," said Mills, who has sold many banjos that combine crucial prewar parts with topline replacements for tone rings, necks, and fingerboards.

Among their many parts, bluegrass banjos have several specific elements that are considered key to the banjo's sound.

The Tone Ring: The definitive piece of equipment on a Mastertone is the tone ring, a circular metal part that fits on top of the banjo's wood rim and supports the head. When the resonator is in place, a "tone chamber" is created by the head, tone ring, rim, and resonator. As banjo maker Greg Deering put it, "The tone ring of a banjo is the heart or the basis of the sound of a banjo. . . . The wood in the rim and neck affects the color, warmth or brightness of the sound, but the tone ring really determines the basic voice or character of the banjo."[4]

The tone ring is what makes a Mastertone a Mastertone. An optimum, original, high-profile, prewar flathead tone ring, weighing about three pounds and with no banjo attached, is worth roughly the same as a nicely equipped new Toyota Camry.

Researchers and manufacturers have spent decades in efforts to reproduce the exact metallurgical composition of these pieces. However, to round out a discussion of the importance of tone rings, remember that some of Earl Scruggs's powerful groundbreaking banjo work during his days with Bill Monroe, on records and on the Grand Ole Opry, was performed on an RB-11—a good prewar Gibson, but one with *no* tone ring. That points to one of the real secrets of instruments, vintage or not: great musicians can make almost any instrument sound exceptional, simply through the magic in their fingers.

Even people familiar with the basic banjo elements—rim or shell, resonator, neck, fingerboard, bridge, strings, tuners, and more—can quickly get lost in the intricacies of a vintage Mastertone. Skipping over many details, here are some other key elements:

The resonator: The wooden, shallow, removable outside or back of the banjo's body is the resonator. Its purpose is to project the instrument's sound outward. It can be made from a variety of woods. It can be plainly finished or decorated with paint, carving, inlay, or other adornments. The Granada resonator has an admired curly maple veneer over a laminated poplar core.

The flange: A metal connector, subject to countless variations from manufacturer to manufacturer, that attaches the banjo's resonator to the rim. Scruggs's Granada has a one-piece flange which, with its associated thinner rim and full-weight flathead tone ring (whose manufacture began at about the same time the one-piece flange was introduced) is the most sought-after configuration.

The rim: On banjos without resonators, the variety played by Pete Seeger or in old-time music, the round wooden rim forms the outside of the instrument. With the head installed, it looks somewhat like a tambourine. The rim on a vintage Mastertone is multi-ply maple with an 11-inch outside diameter.

The head: The head is the round piece once made of hide, now more usually Mylar plastic, which is tightened over the rim. The bridge rests on the head, and strings cross the bridge to be secured by a tailpiece. The term "flathead" means that the head has no elevation; it stretches straight across the rim. That distinguishes it from the style called a "raised head" or "archtop," on which the head's surface angles down toward the rim near its edge.

These differences between the flathead and the raised head result from the different shapes of the tone rings. Some great players, such as Ralph Stanley, Doug Dillard, and Allen Shelton, have preferred the raised-head banjo and its sound. An original 5-string raised-head Mastertone would be welcome at Banjothon, but it is the flatheads that get the attention.

"I prefer the flat-top," Scruggs said. "The main thing I have noticed in the sound of the flat-top, as opposed to the archtop, is that it has more depth in most banjos. You might say it's like a 12-inch speaker compared to a 10-inch one. I prefer a deep, mellow tone; however, you will notice variations in either type of tone chamber."

≡≡≡

Scruggs's RB-11 fell apart after much use when the Blue Grass Boys played a show in a rainstorm. Next, Scruggs played and recorded with a 1938 Gibson RB-75, the one he was to trade to Don Reno at WCYB.[5]

As mentioned, the Granada that Scruggs acquired from Reno was in less than prime condition. But after he had the damage repaired and set the banjo up to suit his playing style, his Granada and the sound he produced on it became the standard by which all other bluegrass banjos are generally judged.

News of desirable prewar Mastertones that are located and snagged spreads in a variety of ways, though typically not in widely circulated media. There are spots in the cyber world, such as "Collector's Corner" on the website Banjo Hangout, where news of buying and selling appears. Owners' names are often either unknown or left unsaid.

≡≡≡

Within a few blocks along Eighth Avenue South near downtown Nashville are two of the world's preeminent dealers in vintage instruments, Gruhn Guitars and Carter Vintage Instruments. George Gruhn has had a vintage-instrument shop in Nashville since 1970 and is regarded as an authority on prewar stringed instruments.

Gruhn and two friends started the store under the name GTR. The letters stood for Gruhn, Dobro player and collector Tut Taylor, and instrument maker Randy Wood. During the later 1960s, Gruhn noted, bluegrass players and collectors favored several topline, prewar instruments worth significant amounts: A big Martin D-28 guitar, a Gibson F-5 mandolin like the one Bill Monroe played, and Scruggs's choice, a Gibson Mastertone banjo.

Players and collectors began to assemble a body of knowledge about these instruments. In the first two decades after the recording of "Foggy Mountain Breakdown," banjo collecting and trading mostly occurred among small circles of true believers. Before information flowed easily on the internet, seekers discovered lore at concerts and festivals, at a few music stores, and in the few bluegrass-themed publications. Pioneers in the Carolinas, such as Mack Crowe and Harry West, who later moved to New York City, traded and sold vintage instruments. Other well-known early traders were Tut Taylor, Harry West, Harry Sparks, and Curtis McPeake. Roger Sprung, John Bernunzio, Stan Jay, and others kept an eye out in the Northeast. At his "Banjo Ranch" in Florida, D. D. Yokeley was another of the very early collectors.

Scruggs himself, and acolytes such as J. D. Crowe and Sonny Osborne, mined the hinterlands for outstanding prewar banjos while on tour. Amateurs were also out looking for the instrument of their dreams. In 1967, a young man named Gene Knight bought a prewar flathead for $400 from a bulletin-board listing at North Carolina State University in Raleigh. He still has it and plays it on gigs.

"They were very cheap compared to what they are now," Gruhn said in fall 2015, seated in the upstairs office of his three-story empire between downtown Nashville and Music Row.

"Prior to the folk boom, hardly anyone was really looking for them. There were a few bluegrassers looking, but they just paid a few hundred dollars for them. Keep in mind that in 1950, a 1935 banjo was just 15 years old."

Determined efforts to learn more about the original instruments grew along with the rise of vintage dealers such as GTR, Matt Umanov in New York City, Jon Lundberg, and Mandolin Brothers. Given the ups and downs of the instrument business, there had been little comprehensive effort to keep track of the many changes in models, let alone the exact weight and construction of tone rings and other lore that is now cherished.

"You could talk to ex-Gibson employees," Gruhn said. "The other thing you could do was look at old Gibson catalogs. In the '60s, the '30s weren't that long ago. Some of the stores still had them."

Trained as a herpetologist—cages containing snakes and lizards still line the walls of his office—Gruhn took a systematic approach to the work of documenting instruments.

However, a lot of the early information that passed from collector to collector turned out to be wrong, Gruhn said. Close-up examinations became key.

"You could look at banjos that you knew to be original and compare," Gruhn said.

Prices for collectible banjos and other vintage instruments continued to rise through about the mid-1970s, flagging when baby boomers' needs for homes, baby clothes, and daily sustenance outpaced their desire for great old instruments, Gruhn said. In the 1990s, prices peaked again, putting many instruments out of reach for most working musicians.

≡

Down the street toward downtown Nashville from Gruhn Guitars stands Carter Vintage Guitars, owned by Walter and Christie Carter, a husband and wife who are both former Gruhn employees. North Carolina native Walter Carter was a songwriter and former newspaperman when he teamed up with Gruhn, getting schooled in vintage instruments and writing with Gruhn some of the most highly regarded books and articles in the field. Like Gruhn's, Carter Vintage is full of many instrumental treasures in addition to collectible Gibson banjos.

The same vintage instruments Gruhn mentioned as early collector favorites—prewar dreadnought-sized Martins, F-5 mandolins, and specific Mastertones—retain their status today. Visitors won't often see "goodies" such as these on public showroom walls; they usually stay in more secure rooms for examination by serious purchasers. In many cases, next-level deals have been completed for a high-end item before a dealer buys it. The dealer locates a rare instrument for sale, makes a few phone calls, and buys and sells the instrument without its once being listed or hung on a showroom wall.

That was true of the Mastertone that an Alabama family sold to Carter Vintage in 2015. "We sold it later that day," Walter Carter said. This banjo is historic. It bears the factory order number 9475-1 and is the first 20-hole-ring, one-piece flange flathead RB-Granada that Gibson produced, according to banjo picker and historian Brent Lamons.

Most valuations concentrate on date, condition, originality, and other such tangible data. Collectors who find banjos meeting all the desired specifications buy them even if they don't sound great, believing that these instruments can almost certainly be set up for exceptional sound.

Walter Carter said: "I see this when good players come in and find the voice of the instrument, and they bring it out."

Dealers have to stay on top of the most intensively researched lore, using latter-day sources such as *Spann's Guide to Gibson 1902–1941*. This can mean examining and reexamining original source material in the light of latter-day analysis. For example, Joe Spann, Gibson expert on staff at Gruhn Guitars, casts doubt on the 1932 Gibson catalog's use of terms such as "quadruple gold plated" and the Granada's "triple gold plating."

"Such terms have little or no significance in the real world of the electroplating industry and were no doubt originated in Gibson's advertising department," Spann wrote.

In the small world of vintage Mastertones, everything gets tough scrutiny because the difference between a prewar with an original tone ring and one with a modern replacement ring, or with a replacement neck instead of an original 5-string neck, amounts to many thousands of dollars.

"It's probably the most difficult instrument to authenticate as 'all original,' mostly because there are so many parts," Carter said. However, there's another side to the "originality" equation. With full disclosure, it is possible to put together high-performing banjos with character and desirability from key pieces of different prewar banjos coupled with newly made necks and even rigorously manufactured new tone rings.

＝＝＝

Conversions of this sort are often mulled over at banjo get-togethers. In October 2015, Mills's seminar drew a few dozen people to the showroom in the basement of his home near Raleigh, North Carolina. The banjo room is fitted with leather furniture and glass display cases. It looks as though it could be a salesroom for fine clothing or jewelry. Mills and his wife, Kim, made a day of it for the attendees, starting with coffee and pastries, as group members chatted and renewed old acquaintances.

There was no podium or microphone once the event got started. Mills and guests sat on chairs amid a collection of instruments, parts, posters, photographs, and other memorabilia related to Gibson instruments and bluegrass music.

Said Mills, "Nineteen-twenty-five and 1926 is where we're going to start."

He took the group through a comprehensive history of the instruments, illustrating points with the several original flatheads in his own collection. Along the way, he imparted the results of his research and personal stories of his friendships with Scruggs, J. D. Crowe, Sonny Osborne and many others. He pointed out that until the late 1950s, banjos had calfskin heads, which required constant attention based on changes in temperature and humidity.

"These guys had to be major mechanics on a banjo," Mills said. "Earl Scruggs in my opinion was one of the greatest. When he got through with a show, he would loosen the strings of the banjo and lay the bridge down. The next day it would take him 30 to 40 minutes to set the banjo back up."

Another of the attractions for Mills's visitors was his artistry as a player. At different points during the day, he'd take one or another of his personal collection of original flatheads, or a high-level prewar conversion model, and animate such tunes as "Hot Corn, Cold Corn," "Roll On, Buddy," "Reuben," and "You Don't Know My Mind."

In the 1,000-square-foot room, with no amplification and no accompaniment, the banjos reached every ear with full articulation and range of frequencies. Mills, like other banjo intellectuals, has thought hard about the context of these instruments, including the way they were designed to roar in a premicrophone era.

"Their main goal in all musical manufacturing at the time was volume," he said. Mills, a multiple-year winner of the International Bluegrass Music Association's Banjo Player of the Year award, brought out the deep clarity of the banjos' lowest string, called the bass string and typically tuned to a D or a C. The midranges rolled like a Carolina river, and the higher-end notes descended like glistening sunrays, with none of the harshness of an amplified instrument. It was easy, hearing an original flathead or high-end conversion taken through its paces, to imagine shelling out a fortune or spending years trolling attics and closets for an object of such art and utility.

Attendee Michael McCartney, 66, got into vintage banjos after playing part-time for decades while working as a physician's assistant. Following a suggestion that Mills makes frequently, McCartney opted for a "conversion," spending $6,500, including strap and case, for a banjo that left the factory in 1930 as Gibson TB-1, or four-string tenor banjo. It didn't originally have a tone ring but was adaptable to having one installed. Equipped with a five-string neck and high-quality modern tone ring, the instrument gave McCartney, now retired, a great-sounding "prewar Gibson" for a fraction of the price of an original five-string.

"I don't take that one out of the house," he said during a break in the seminar.

⸺

Time spent at the Banjothon conventions is less structured than at Mills's seminar. People who own one or sometimes several of these great banjos typically come in the night before, checking in at the same downtown Knoxville hotel and engaging in late-night picking and talking. Once proceedings get going on a Saturday morning, the event becomes a kaleidoscopic combination of bluegrass festival, swap meet, revival, and family reunion. Representatives of dealers such as Mills, Gruhn, and Elderly Instruments have intimidating collections of instruments roped off around the edges of the room, while pickers like Gene Knight show up with one great banjo in hand.

Banjothon is in some ways defined by what it's not. Sales may be quietly discussed, but it's not a sale or swap meet. It's OK to ask permission to take a banjo off its stand and pick it to get an idea of its sound, but no one is to start a jam session on the exhibit floor, especially not in the morning.

"It's like a Corvette show, just show and tell," said organizer Larry Mathis.

Although well-known pickers show up, Banjothon mostly draws people who might be called Mastertone superfans. They spend hours on online sites such as "Collector's Corner," asking questions, offering opinions, and debating fine points of desirable banjos. The first Banjothon, organized by Mathis in 2000, drew only eight people, but the numbers kept increasing; 165 invitees attended by 2014, and the numbers kept growing

Stars in this musical field make appearances, as well as preeminent collectors, allowing attendees to gather a wealth of banjo lore. Eddie Adcock, known for his work with the Country Gentlemen and in a duo with Martha Hearon Adcock, came several times in recent years to swap stories and banjo wisdom even when he was using an oxygen tank at the time because of long-term health problems. "When I started playing I didn't think I'd ever play as good as Earl or some of the banjo players at the time," said Adcock, who was to incorporate Merle Travis fingerpicking, steel guitar, and single-note jazz into his banjo style. "Being a farm boy and having the feeling of not being able to measure up, I didn't try to do anything anybody else was doing. I went my own route and it kind of paid off."

===

Sonny Osborne, banjo royalty since his long partnership with mandolin-playing brother Bobby, sat in a high-backed chair at Banjothon like a potentate of old.

"I studied everything I could," Sonny, retired as an Osborne Brother, said of his early days of learning bluegrass on the banjo. "After a while, I got to the point where I could do that stuff. Earl just played it naturally and it came out like that. There was nothing like it then, and there still isn't today."

Collector Darrell McCumbers, who tells attendees he's sold 29 original flatheads, approached to show Osborne a vintage Vega that Osborne once owned. McCumbers had a large display of his own banjos a few feet away. A West Virginia native, McCumbers became fascinated with Scruggs when he started hearing him on the radio in the late 1940s. "They said Earl's using picks," he recalled, referring to Scruggs's virtually unprecedented use of a plastic thumb pick and metal fingerpicks on the banjo.

When he retired in 1976, McCumbers started serious collecting and dealing, hitting the road and asking for leads on instruments wherever he and his wife went.

"We just drive around looking for any old instruments," he said.

One afternoon at Banjothon, Greg Earnest, an authority and keeper of the Prewar Gibson Mastertone Banjos website, turned up in a side room with some other enthusiasts who were trying out instruments away from the informal restrictions of the main space.

"This is an original flathead," he said of a banjo he'd brought. "An instrument like this is the holy grail."

When picking began, "Foggy Mountain Breakdown" was one of the first tunes played.

"I've never gotten tired of it," Earnest said after rendering the instrumental while joined only by a couple of other banjoists. "I've been a student of Scruggs since I was a kid."

15

REAPING THE HARVEST

By the 1990s, the thirst for American roots music was freshening. New fans were coming to the sound through acts like bluegrass-reared country star Ricky Skaggs, who built much of his style on Monroe, Flatt and Scruggs, and the Stanley Brothers. Fiddler and vocalist Alison Krauss, whose early bluegrass favorites were J. D. Crowe and the New South, was becoming the genre's best-selling star. Instrumental prodigies such as Béla Fleck, Jerry Douglas, and Sam Bush worked together as well as heading up their own outfits, combining their knowledge of hard-core bluegrass with quirky mixes of jazz, rock, world, and classical music. The vintage banjo boom was still growing. Obsessed young people joined obsessed older people in chasing the few Mastertones perhaps still hiding in closets.

Into this context, Earl Scruggs reemerged during the '90s and into the 2000s from what some had called a retirement in the 1980s. People who traced "roots music" soon discovered that Scruggs, an intellectual and commercial leader of this music, was still very much around and remained a primary source of the "old tones" people were seeking. Scruggs had been part of the enduring transformation of Southeastern country string-band music. He was willing to share his memories and theories about what had happened and about his role in it. His later years took on a sort of king-of-the-mountain character as U.S. presidents, movie stars, arts supporters, and cultural leaders wanted to honor or just be around Scruggs, joining the many musicians who found their way to his work.

Among the influential followers who helped keep Scruggs's music front and center were Steve Martin, the A-list actor-comedian-musician, and Fleck, the banjo virtuoso who seemed to come closest to matching Scruggs's original burst of banjo creativity. Adding to the banjo's growing popularity, the latest generation of Scruggs-influenced players arrived, including Jim Mills, Rob McCoury, Mike Munford, Alison Brown, Noam Pikelny, and Kristin Scott Benson. Brown, the eclectic banjo star, Harvard-educated founder of Compass Records, and former investment banker, placed *Foggy Mountain Banjo* first on her list when asked for her Top 10 favorite albums. "Foggy Mountain Breakdown" continued to attract new cuts from a far-ranging list of pickers. Just a few of them were Martin, country star Hank Williams Jr., folk-rockers the Nitty Gritty Dirt Band, the Brazilian bluegrass band Trem 27, "Deliverance" recording artist Eric Weissberg, rockabilly revivalists the Stray Cats, and *Andy Griffith Show* regular and notable picker Doug Dillard.

Scruggs clearly had a large-scale legacy to show for his decades of work. Countless bluegrass bands had a banjo player who also sang baritone harmony, largely because Scruggs had taken that part in Flatt and Scruggs. If bluegrass music had been a movie, Scruggs would have created the role of the banjo player who played great, didn't say much, but showed a wry sense of humor when he did. Setbacks of various sorts would continue, but the last two decades of Scruggs's life often found him covered in glory.

It was about time. Going back to the 1950s, he had had a crushing share of physical ailments, including a devastating 1955 car wreck, a 1975 plane crash, and the general toll of aging. One day in 1996, Scruggs had entered the hospital for a hip replacement, endured a heart attack while in recovery, and then went through successful quintuple bypass surgery.

Tragedy hit hardest when Steve Scruggs, Louise and Earl's youngest son and longtime member of the Revue, killed his wife and then took his own life in 1992. Earl Scruggs reportedly took a year away from the banjo. But that turned out not to be the ideal road to recovery, he told an interviewer a decade later.

"I just can't live in a depressed world too long," Scruggs said. "To get out of that, I just have to get the banjo and start playing."

Honors and awards continued to come Scruggs's way, some recognizing him alone and others his duet work with Lester Flatt, including the original recording of "Foggy Mountain Breakdown" and its 1969 Grammy recognition. Governor James B. Hunt Jr. of North Carolina declared January 6, 1984, Earl's 60th birthday, Earl Scruggs Day in the state. President Ronald Reagan and his wife Nancy sent him a congratulatory telegram. On October 14, 1985, Flatt and Scruggs won induction into the Country Music Hall of Fame on the same night that major fan Ricky Skaggs won the Country Music Association's top award, Entertainer of the Year. Scruggs showed up for the ceremony at the Grand Ole Opry. "I didn't have a speech prepared that night," he said later. "I just went up and smiled and bowed and walked off. From the way I'm rattlin' off now it doesn't sound like it, but put me out on a stage to make a speech and I just go speechless."[1]

Membership in the Hall of Fame puts an act in the company of the first three members—Jimmie Rodgers, the Carter Family, and business giant Ralph Peer—among dozens of additional influential musicians and business people. Scruggs would also win the National Heritage Fellowship from the National Endowment for the Arts in 1989.

President George W. Bush presented Scruggs with the National Medal of Arts in 1992; Scruggs's friend and Opry colleague Minnie Pearl received the same honor that day.

Then there were inductions with Flatt into the Grammy Hall of Fame, first for the Mercury single of "Foggy Mountain Breakdown" in 1999 and later for two albums, *Foggy Mountain Banjo* in 2011 and *Foggy Mountain Jamboree* in 2013.

In 2000, honors came from National Public Radio, which named "Foggy Mountain Breakdown" one of the 100 most important American musical works of the 20th century. In 2003, a star in his honor was installed on the Hollywood Walk of Fame. On April 5, 2005, Librarian of Congress James H. Billington named "Foggy Mountain Breakdown" to the National Recording Registry, denoting recordings that are "culturally, historically or aesthetically significant." (Full disclosure: Years later I wrote, by request and without pay, an article about "Foggy Mountain Breakdown" that appears online with its National Recording Registry listing.)

The Earl Scruggs Revue had disbanded in 1982 after more than a decade of successful performing, recording, and touring. When Scruggs went back to steady work in the 1990s, it was to lead a group usually known as Earl Scruggs, Family and Friends. Gary and Randy came back. Additional accomplished players such as fiddler Glen Duncan, mandolin star Sam Bush, Dobro players Jerry Douglas and Rob Ickes, guitarist-mandolinist John Jorgenson, and drummers John Gardner and Harry Stinson were part of the troupe at different times.

"To get to play music with the person who inspired me to play music in the first place—what could be better than that?" Douglas said.[2]

The continued presence of a drummer in the band still caused some concern among hard-core fans who regarded bluegrass as a style that created plenty of drive without a separate percussionist. East Tennessee native John Gardner, a highly regarded drummer with plenty of roots-music credibility, said in an email he had his own concerns until he happened to overhear Scruggs in conversation with an interviewer.

"I was about to exit the bus at one gig while Earl was doing a radio interview in the front lounge," said Gardner, who played with the group for nine years. "I heard the interviewer ask him, 'Why do you use a drummer?' Of course I froze to hear his reply. He sat there thinking for some time then said, 'Well, let me put it this way. I'll never work without one.'"[3]

In contrast with some drummers who have used a "swung," or dotted-note approach that can conflict with the straight time of bluegrass, Gardner made most frequent use of straight sixteenth notes. After all, that's most often the time that Scruggs would be keeping.

"From the time I started with Earl, I always used brushes," Gardner said. "There were some songs that were played in sixteenth-note half-time, but the majority of songs were sixteenth-note, what I call two-beat or 'train' feel. There were subtle variations but basically all were sixteenth-note feel."

Jerry Douglas, while noting his respect for Gardner's musicianship, opposed the notion of having drums in the band. "Earl should have been the drums," he said.

═══

In July 1994, Scruggs was definitely picking intensely again, in company that could have reflected old tensions, even as it recalled great moments in bluegrass. Ricky Skaggs was playing one of a series of bluegrass shows at downtown Nashville's Ryman Auditorium, a former home of the Grand Ole Opry that was seeing increased use for Opry and other shows. The shows were designed to have a special feel about them, and Skaggs invited his heroes Bill Monroe and Earl Scruggs to join him on stage.[4] With rock-steady session bass man Roy Huskey Jr. and former Blue Grass Boys fiddler Benny Martin completing the group, it was almost as close as the 1990s could offer to a reunion of the classic Blue Grass Boys lineup. (Lester Flatt and Howard Watts died in the '70s, but Chubby Wise would live until 1996.)

And the band blazed. Skaggs, in the Flatt role, started off as lead vocalist on Lester and Monroe's composition, "Will You Be Loving Another Man," with Scruggs singing baritone and Monroe tenor. When it was time for a picking tune, what should come up but "Blue Grass Breakdown"? As previously discussed, this was the instrumental that both Monroe and Scruggs claimed to have written, just as both claimed principal credit for "Foggy Mountain Breakdown." All that seemed to be in the past. Monroe had his name on "Blue Grass Breakdown," Scruggs was the established creator of "Foggy Mountain Breakdown," and the world of bluegrass was the winner, at least for this night.

Monroe started at full breakdown speed on the mandolin, Scruggs matched the tempo when it was his turn to pick, and Martin threw his trademark wild licks into the mix. Both Monroe, 82, and Scruggs, 70, dominated their instruments like men in the prime of life. After just a few more songs—one of them was "Reuben," Scruggs's first three-finger creation—the reunion concluded.

"I'm so glad we're all friends together," Monroe said when it was over.

Both Scruggs and Monroe recognized the value of what country singer Clint Black once referred to as "a good old friendly fight."

"You know you've got competition in bluegrass music," Monroe once said. "If you play a banjo number the best you can play it, the next man out there is going to play it hard. You've got people out there like Earl Scruggs and Don Reno to face, and you'd better come with the best that you've got or you're not going to sell."[5]

On these later-era "and Friends" gigs, "Foggy Mountain Breakdown" got a full ride every night. Scruggs considered the banjo number to be at the heart of his work as a musician.

"It's hard to get a piece of music, for anybody, that'll become a standard like that one," he said. "I've written other tunes I thought was better than that, but it didn't do nothing to what 'Foggy Mountain Breakdown' did, and nobody has the answer to it.

"It just fit in where it was played. And I always thought the movie hit did an awful lot for it. But, you know, the movie came and gone and it's still going good, 'Foggy Mountain Breakdown' is."

Scruggs was talking in 2007, in the pristine white living room of his capacious home on Franklin Road in Nashville. Forty years had passed since the release of *Bonnie and Clyde*, Scruggs was pointing out, so all the tune's popularity couldn't be laid to that movie. Many fans hadn't been born when the movie came out, he said. I asked him if it still got a big response when the band played it on the road.

"Mm-hmm, it sure does," he said.

That was a classic Scruggs moment. He never boasted, to my knowledge, but he must have seen in other people's eyes, and in their music, the effect that he had on those who followed him. Scruggs remained generous and friendly, back to the days when he'd given a random visitor some pointers at a Nashville hotel despite Bill Monroe's suspicions. That welcoming attitude also emerged in the relationship he developed with Béla Fleck, the player who, after Scruggs, has done the most to elevate and diversify the banjo's image.

After being introduced to Scruggs by John Hartford, Fleck became a frequent visitor at Scruggs's home. At first he did his best to play like Scruggs. Then Fleck realized that Scruggs thoroughly enjoyed the wild tonalities and rhythmic excursions that Fleck added to the music.

"He would smile when I'd do it," Fleck said.

≡

Earl and Louise Scruggs used to describe wonderingly the musicians from Japan and other far-flung places who showed up at Donna Drive in Madison or on Franklin Road in Nashville.

The couple held legendary parties at their house, where relatives, bluegrass founders, country stars, and others gathered for big spreads of food and picking sessions. There was speculation that the hip and knee surgery Scruggs went through left him feeling better, and he certainly entered a highly productive period.

Louise, whom Earl met in 1946 and married in 1948, continued to handle business affairs for whatever act her husband joined or created. She had a diverse, specific vision for the kind of projects that would suit him.

The energy and accessibility of Scruggs's compositions made them naturals for use in movies, television, and advertising. These included the appearance of "Foggy Mountain Breakdown" in such unlikely offerings as *Penguins of Madagascar*, 2014; *The Office*, 2012; *The Love Guru*, 2008; *Moonlighting*, 1989; *Hot Dallas Nights*, 1981; *The Tycoon's Daughter*, 1973; and, perhaps most oddly, *Monty Python's Flying Circus*, in 1971.

As far as personal appearances, being choosy about performances meant Scruggs was more likely to show up on David Letterman's late-night television show than at a string of bluegrass festivals.

≡

On November 15, 2001, Steve Martin helped publicize Scruggs's star-studded album *Earl Scruggs & Friends* by appearing on Letterman's show for a new version of "Foggy Mountain Breakdown" using players from the studio recording. They included Douglas, star fiddler Glen Duncan, bluegrass-loving country stars Vince Gill and Marty Stuart, rock-country shredder Albert Lee, Gary Scruggs, Randy Scruggs, *Late Night* bandleader Paul Shaffer, and drummer Harry Stinson. Only Leon Russell on organ was missing from the big-band lineup heard on the disc.

"A video of us playing along with the recorded track was released and went to the Number 4 spot on the CMT cable channel video chart," Gary Scruggs said.

Not only that, the arrangement, at the other end of the spectrum from the no-frills 1949 version, won a second Grammy for "Foggy Mountain Breakdown." No other pop tune had twice won one of the coveted awards for the same artist.

The heavily electrified version was unlikely to please hard-core bluegrassers, but the industry recognition for Scruggs was regarded as well deserved. The album with the "Foggy Mountain Breakdown" remake also featured guest performances from pop artists such as Elton John, Don Henley, Sting, Melissa Etheridge, and movie star Billy Bob Thornton. The Grammy award came the same year that the breakthrough *O Brother, Where Art Thou?* dominated the awards show, kicking the roots-music boom up several notches in volume.

In 2005, Martin arranged a repeat Letterman performance with a group called "Men with Banjos (Who Know How to Use Them)." Comprised of Martin, Scruggs, Hot Rize's Pete Wernick, former Blue Grass Boy Tony Ellis, and Charles Wood, the pickers whipped through "Foggy Mountain Breakdown" with help from accompanists including pianist Shaffer. Martin made sure that all the banjoists had their names called when Letterman came out to congratulate them.

New versions of "Foggy Mountain Breakdown" kept on coming, sometimes in striking approaches, such as the one performed by the celebrated finger-style guitarist Muriel Anderson, who had played bluegrass in her youth. In a medley with the Stephen Foster–derived fiddle tune "Angeline the Baker," Anderson nailed "Foggy Mountain Breakdown," bent notes and all. In a Facebook post after Scruggs died, Anderson recalled performing it at the Scruggses' 50th wedding anniversary celebration.

"When I played his notes of 'Foggy Mountain Breakdown' on classical guitar, he started leaning in closer and closer until his nose was inches from my left hand," she wrote.[6]

Louise Certain Scruggs, Earl's wife and guiding star for 58 years, died on February 2, 2006. Earl and Louise Scruggs had been inseparable—from their first exchange of glances at the Ryman Auditorium, through the years of living and raising boys in trailers and apartments, to settling in fine Nashville homes. Pete Wernick, a key figure as a banjo player, teacher and IBMA leader, wrote about Louise's funeral on his "Notes from the Road" blog:[7]

"Grand Ole Opry announcer, music historian, and fiddler extraordinaire Eddie Stubbs served as informative master of ceremonies, recounting highlights of Louise's life and introducing a number of speakers and performers. Several of Louise's favorite songs were performed, 'In the Garden,' by Dwight Yoakam, 'I Walk the Line' by Travis Tritt, and 'Go Rest High' by Vince Gill."

The closeness of Earl and Louise extended beyond their personal life into the careers of every act from Flatt and Scruggs on.

"My mother became the booking agent for F&S beginning in 1955 and continued to do so until they disbanded in 1969," according to Gary, who managed Earl after Louise's death. "She was also the manager for F&S during those years. She was the first female artist manager and booking agent in the history of country music. She then continued to manage Dad's career until her passing."

—————

A glitzy California event brought Scruggs back into the orbit of Warren Beatty, whose use of Scruggs's picking in *Bonnie and Clyde* started its arc of wider recognition.

Recalled Gary Scruggs, "Early in 2008, a representative for the American Film Institute (AFI) in Los Angeles, California, contacted me to tell me that the AFI was going to present Warren Beatty with a Lifetime Achievement Award later in that year. That special award show would be taped for broadcast on cable TV (the USA Channel), and the plan called for the show to begin with a few-minutes-long collage of film clips in which Warren had appeared—then, Warren would be introduced and come out on stage and then descend into the theater's floor and make his way through the crowd to his Table of Honor.

"I was excited to learn that Warren had made a request that Dad play 'Foggy Mountain Breakdown' during his introduction. I ran the proposal by Dad, and he immediately agreed to accept the invitation."

The event took place on the evening on June 12, 2008, in the Kodak Theater in Hollywood, with Scruggs backed by Gary on bass, fiddler Hoot Hester, guitarists Randy Scruggs and Jon Randall, and drummer Gardner.[8]

"We were positioned on stage right, and Warren entered the stage from stage left when Dad kicked off 'Foggy Mountain Breakdown,'" Gary said. "The atmosphere in the room was electric. A few seconds after Warren entered the stage, he waved to Dad, and even though Dad was picking, Dad waved back with his left hand as his right hand continued to pick. Warren then approached Dad and extended his right hand as if to shake hands.

"Dad was still busy picking 'Foggy Mountain Breakdown,' so in order not to break the flow of the picking, Dad extended his left hand and kept picking with his right hand. Instead of shaking Dad's left hand, Warren bent down and kissed Dad's left hand and patted it. It was a fun moment and the respect the two men had for one another was obvious."

The Scruggs family and friends kept the music going as Beatty, 70, made his way through a glitzy throng that included *Bonnie and Clyde* co-star Faye Dunaway; Beatty's sister Shirley MacLaine; Beatty's wife, Annette Bening;

Diane Keaton; Jack Nicholson; and Dustin Hoffman. During Beatty's long approach, "Foggy Mountain Breakdown" raged on.

"The tune lasted for at least six minutes, perhaps even closer to seven minutes, which was pretty tiring considering the tune's tempo," Gary said.

Amid speeches by many other celebrities, Dunaway presented her remarks at the tribute in the same sort of amateurish poetry that Bonnie Parker had composed in the 1930s for the public benefit. "I'm his Bonnie, he's my Clyde," said Dunaway, 66, once more reciting as Parker.

Years later, in what might have been a final reprise of the off-kilter exploits of Bonnie and Clyde, Beatty and Dunaway went astray from their duties when they agreed to present the Best Picture award at the 2017 Academy Awards. In a slipup that the pair blamed on one another, Dunaway took an envelope from Beatty and then incorrectly announced that *La La Land* had won, when the real winner was *Moonlight*. On February 26, 2017, *Variety* reporters Dave McNary and Alex Steadman called the blunder "the most chaotic conclusion to the Academy Awards ever."

Steve Martin has had notable success as a standup comic, recording artist, bankable movie star, playwright, and essayist. In recent years, he's taken up a new gig—touring, recording, and playing skilled, mostly Scruggs-style banjo with the North Carolina–based bluegrass band Steep Canyon Rangers and rock-pop singer Edie Brickell. When Martin talks about Scruggs, his friend for decades, he shows the same mix of awe and fondness displayed by Scruggs's other fans and admirers.

Like countless players, Martin had his banjo switch turned to the "on" position by hearing tunes such as "Foggy Mountain Breakdown," as well as others on the *Foggy Mountain Banjo* LP. He was a Southern California high school student at the time, with a standup comedy gig in his future.

"'Foggy Mountain Breakdown' was like a turbocharger to one's interest in the banjo,"[9] Martin said. "It was the first place I really heard three-finger Scruggs style. I can't quite remember how much it preceded me hearing the Dillards. All of these things really coalesced over a year or less."

Martin went to high school with John McEuen of the Nitty Gritty Dirt Band, who gave bluegrass a boost with their *Will the Circle Be Unbroken* double album a few years later.

"John McEuen took me down to La Jolla in California, and we went backstage and met Earl," Martin said. "Earl was so likable and so friendly. He showed me how to play 'Sally Goodin' exactly like him. I recorded it; it's just me alone. It was on the back of 'King Tut.'"

"Sally Goodin" has been a staple of fiddlers and banjo players since long before Texan Eck Robertson recorded it in 1922. It's quite a leap from there to the 45 rpm release of the eccentric 1978 hit "King Tut," debuted by Martin in the great days of *Saturday Night Live*. The novelty tune, with backing by the Dirt Band as the "Toot Uncommons," became a hit record. In pop culture, it seems, Earl Scruggs has quite often been at the center, or just a B side's distance, from whatever's going on. Recently, Martin revived "King Tut" in a bluegrass-y version with the Steep Canyon Rangers.

Once stereotyped in show business as a "wild and crazy guy," Martin remains serious in conversation. His banjo playing became a notable prop of his comedy act, he said, but not on purpose.

"I never thought of it, or used it, as a funny instrument," he said. "I used it in my act because my act looked ad lib and made up, so if I played the banjo, it looked like I could do something."

Martin clung to his love of bluegrass while growing in experience and show-business stature. He had learned banjo the old-fashioned way, by turning a vinyl LP of Flatt and Scruggs to a slower speed and puzzling over the licks until he got them. The *Live at Carnegie Hall* album, with its duet between Scruggs and fiddler Paul Warren, was a favorite.

"One of the most potent songs for me was the one they called 'Fiddle and Banjo,'" he said. "I just loved that sound, the rolling banjo and the fiddle and nothing else, so expressive and so emotional." He still tuned in to Scruggs's recording when he heard them on the radio or streaming on a computer. He has had other obligations, serving twice as host and once as co-host of the Academy Awards telecast and starring in more than 30 movies.

Martin got back on a bluegrass roll in the early 2000s, partly as a result of satellite radio, where the general availability of bluegrass acts from several eras reawakened his interest, he said as he accepted a Distinguished Achievement Award from the International Bluegrass Music Association in 2015 in Raleigh. This was also the period in which he helped promote Scruggs's comeback, simply through star-powered friendship.

"I heard Earl Scruggs, and that was the epiphany that not only I but so many people in this room had," Martin said upon accepting the award.

Fleck was commissioned to write a banjo concerto to perform with the Nashville Symphony and he worked on it during the year or so before Scruggs died in 2012. The entire process, often wrenching for the composer, was captured in a documentary, *How to Write a Banjo Concerto*, in which Scruggs appeared, listening to the work and consulting as it progressed.

Scruggs showed up for the debut of Fleck's concerto, but that was perhaps his last public appearance. At 88, his health was failing. Steve Martin wrote a piece for *The New Yorker* about Scruggs, lyrically recalling the career of the North Carolina farm boy who had notes "shooting from his fingertips." Martin wrote: "Before him, no one had ever played the banjo like he did. After him, everyone played the banjo like he did, or at least tried."[10]

Because he loved to pick and picked exceedingly well, Scruggs brought about far-reaching change in his nearly nine decades on earth. He created a banjo style, built new respect for the instrument, and made his name on extraordinary creativity, genial temperament, and fair dealing. However, "He wasn't Gandhi," as Fleck said years later, and could nurse grudges and resentments as most humans do.

After his death on March 28, 2012, thousands of fans flocked to the Ryman Auditorium on April 1 in respect and tribute. Musician-broadcaster Eddie Stubbs gave the eulogy, and the list of performers included Fleck, Skaggs, the Whites, Jim Mills, Emmylou Harris, Vince Gill, Marty Stuart, Jon Randall Stewart, John McEuen, and Patty Loveless.

The banjo player Bill Evans wrote on his blog: "As the casket passed up the center aisle of the Ryman Auditorium at the conclusion of a very moving memorial service, I stood with my friends Tony Trischka, Ned Luberecki, Kristin Scott Benson, Alan O'Bryant, Jim Mills, John McEuen, Tim O'Brien, Sam Bush, Alison Brown, Noam Pikelny, Béla Fleck, Richard Bailey and others, honoring Earl by lowering the neck of my 1930 Gibson Granada as he passed through the Ryman one final time."[11]

Succeeding years have shown that Scruggs's death has not diminished his overarching influence on acoustic music and bluegrass. Not long after Scruggs died, Fleck composed and performed a moving 11-minute tribute solo banjo. Fleck knew Scruggs's story inside and out and laid it out musically on his own Mastertone, using tunes such as "You Are My Flower," which Scruggs recorded on guitar; the pop adaptation "Farewell Blues"; the Mack Woolbright-inspired "Home Sweet Home"; the tuner showpiece "Earl's Breakdown"; the blues-boppin' "Foggy Mountain Special"; the chiming "Bugle Call Rag"; and Fleck's own starting place on the banjo, "The Ballad of Jed Clampett." "Foggy Mountain Breakdown" found its place, and a huge ovation, during the piece.

A whole generation of top-level players, and not just banjo players, learned what it meant to be a musician in large part from listening to and, if they were lucky, playing with Earl Scruggs. One of them was Douglas, who had earned his reputation as an inventive, expert Dobro player with bands including the Country Gentlemen and J. D. Crowe and the New South. Since then, his ability has led to gigs and sessions accompanying household names such as Eric Clapton and James Taylor. He's also had an ongoing role as a featured member of Alison Krauss's Union Station band.

═══

What was supposed to be a quick-turn recording session by Jerry Douglas with banjo man Charlie Cushman and fiddler Johnny Warren led to something entirely different. The resulting band, punningly called the Earls of Leicester (pronounced "Lester") in tribute to the classic Flatt and Scruggs sound, has become the most prominent reinforcement of the achievements of Lester Flatt and Earl Scruggs.

"I went over to play on Charlie's record, just kind of playing with them, we kind of turned the guitar off and that was the core of that sound. It was like, 'This is like playing with Flatt and Scruggs,'" Douglas said in 2015.[12]

Cushman had spent the last 40 years in Nashville as an admired Scruggs-style player and banjo craftsman; Warren is the son of Paul Warren, the longest-tenured fiddler for Flatt and Scruggs. Bassist Barry Bales from Krauss's band, eclectic singer-songwriter Tim O'Brien on mandolin, and bluegrass-country singer Shawn Camp got the calls to complete the band. Douglas took on the role of Buck "Uncle Josh" Graves, playing Graves's sweeping, bluesy style to perfection. The band wasn't intended to create exact reproductions of the Foggy Mountain Boys sound, but to remind contemporary audiences of the sound of a real bluegrass band.

"I have been wanting to do it forever, because it was disappearing," Douglas said. "The younger audiences, I see these kids out there—their jaws are on the ground because they are hearing a band sound. And the old-timers come out and say, 'I never thought I'd hear it again.' I get more out of that than anything else."

Released in September 2014, *Jerry Douglas Presents the Earls of Leicester* became a surprise hit, earning a Grammy award and a passel of recognition at the 2014 IBMA awards. The Earls took home awards for the entertainer, album, instrumental group, and gospel recorded performance of the year. Douglas won as Dobro player of the year and Camp was named top male vocalist.

"The Earls thing took off like crazy; I didn't expect that," Douglas said. "It was the power of the Flatt and Scruggs thing behind it that made it happen."

Album cuts such as "Don't Let Your Deal Go Down," "Shuckin' the Corn" and "Dig a Hole in the Meadow" stemmed largely from Flatt and Scruggs's '40s and '50s repertoire.

The popularity of the Earls has revived discussions of exactly how Lester Flatt and Earl Scruggs and their classic band treated acoustic picking and singing as an art form, with intricate interplay of instruments and complex vocal arrangements that take significant work to re-create, Douglas said. A second Flatt-and-Scruggs–based album, "Rattle and Roar," with Jeff White on mandolin, came out in 2016 and earned seven IBMA nominations among the group and individual members.

"It's close enough, but it's not a copy," Fleck said of the Earls. "Those guys are speaking those languages together and it's beautiful."

Douglas and the Earls get down to crucial matters such as the way Scruggs achieved his "drive" on the banjo. Musicians talk about different kinds of timing, in which a player can be slightly behind the beat, dead on the beat, or slightly ahead. As long as the basic tempo stays steady, different approaches can create variety and excitement. Scruggs used to push the beat for all it was worth, Douglas said, while never losing a rock-solid tempo.

The Earls are wont to call on banjo man Cushman for "Foggy Mountain Breakdown" when a gig gets to 11 on the 10-point scale, Douglas said.

"Once in a while when we are having a really good night, we'll do it as an encore," he said. "The place goes nuts; everybody goes crazy."

When the Earls put out their *Live at the CMA Theater* disc in 2018, the 26th and concluding track was "Foggy Mountain Breakdown."

≣

Just as Douglas was forming the Earls of Leicester to keep alive the music of Scruggs's partnership with Flatt, a nonprofit foundation reached its longtime goal of transforming the Cleveland County Courthouse in Shelby, North Carolina, into the Earl Scruggs Center.

Staff at the Center told me that Scruggs was kept up to date on the coming facility and felt awed that the imposing courthouse of his childhood memories was to bear his name. On Saturday, January 11, 2014, family, friends, and fans turned out for ceremonies dedicating the center. John Curtis Goad, writing for *Bluegrass Today*, described the way it came to a conclusion:

"The day finished with a nearly sold-out concert called 'Remembering Earl: Music and Stories' at Shelby High School's Malcolm Brown Auditorium. With Eddie Stubbs as emcee, the evening replicated Scruggs's 'Family and Friends' concerts and featured Rob Ickes, Sam Bush, Jim Mills, Vince Gill, Travis Tritt, John Gardner, and Randy and Gary Scruggs. Throughout the evening, the musicians alternated between songs and memories of Scruggs, reminding the audience of how much Scruggs touched all of our lives."

The center has an ongoing role not just in remembering Scruggs, but also in welcoming Cleveland County natives and visitors to a variety of events with a storytelling theme.

≣

However styles may change, people hunger for music with roots, soul, honesty, and energy. Earl Eugene Scruggs embodied those values as he introduced the world to the worthy banjo picking he heard, then transformed, while still living in the hills near Boiling Springs. Without him, that sound and the five-string banjo would likely have been cast aside. Instead, Scruggs saved them both, leaving music and culture richer for the ages.

NOTES

Chapter 2. "I grew up around a banjo"

1. Betty Jenkins, author telephone interview, March 26, 2015.

2. "Shelby, North Carolina," National Park Service's National Register of Historic Places, www.nps.gov/nr/travel/shelby/history.htm, accessed April 26, 2019.

3. Earl Scruggs, author interview, June 23, 2007.

4. Several states, including North Carolina, did not raise the legal age for marriage from 10 until 1920.

5. Uncredited writer, "George E. Scruggs Died Wednesday," *Forest City Courier*, Forest City, North Carolina, October 12, 1928, 2.

6. Earl Scruggs, author interview, 2007.

7. Gary Scruggs, email interview, August 1, 2015.

8. Dan Collins. "Earl Scruggs: If It Sounded Good, I'd Say 'Let's Do It!'" *LA Record*, Los Angeles, California, April 25, 2009.

9. Uncredited writer, "Earl Scruggs Comes Home," *The Pilot*, Boiling Springs, North Carolina, February 15, 1973, 1.

10. Earl Scruggs, author interview, June 2007.

11. Jack Bernhardt, "Grand Ole Banjo Man: The Man Whose Finger-picking Style Defines Bluegrass Earns a North Carolina Folklife Award on Tuesday Night," *News & Observer*, Raleigh, North Carolina, May 12, 1996, G1.

12. Cleveland County Historical Association book committee, *The Heritage of Cleveland County Vol. 1*, Shelby, North Carolina, 1982, 190–191.

13. Tom Burrus, email interview, September 27, 2015.

Chapter 3. The Piedmont's Rich Musical Soil

1. Pete Peterson, "Getting Started with Charlie Poole Style Banjo," *Old Time Herald*, Vol. 9, Number 8, Summer 2005.

2. Earl Scruggs, author interview, June 2007.

3. Jim Mills, author interview, Durham, North Carolina, March 8, 2013.

4. Tony Trischka, "Snuffy Jenkins," *Bluegrass Unlimited*, October 1977.

5. Uncredited writer, "Seeks to Organize String Musicians," *Gaffney Ledger*, Gaffney, South Carolina, January 11, 1933, 1.

6. Scruggs, author interview, June 2007.

7. Uncredited writer, "Sarratt Given Life Sentence for Murder, Negro Gets Recommendation for Mercy, Godfrey Acquitted," *Gaffney Ledger*, Gaffney, South Carolina, February 6, 1930, 1.

8. Michael Barrett, "He's a Mighty Happy Man," *The Daily Herald*, Chicago, Illinois, October 26, 1973, 33.

9. Bryan DeMarcus, "Ben Humphries," Roots of Rutherford, https://ia801606.us.archive.org/33/items/rootsofrutherforoounse/rootsofrutherforoounse.pdf, accessed April 26, 2019.

10. Joe DePriest, "N.C. to Honor Banjo Legend Scruggs," May 6, 1996, *Charlotte Observer*, 1A.

11. Norman Draper, "The Living Legend Is Still Humble," *The Daily Tar Heel*, Chapel Hill, North Carolina, September 25, 1972, 3.

Chapter 4. Early Professional Days

1. Bill Morrison, "Tar Heel Native Traveled Country Road to Carnegie Hall," *News & Observer*, Raleigh, North Carolina, June 13, 1974, V-3.

2. "Earl Scruggs Benefit Concert Blog," October 11, 2007, *Shelby Star* online edition, Shelby, North Carolina.

3. Morrison, *News and Observer*, June 13, 1974.

4. Joe DePriest, "Fish Fried Perfection; 'Camps Dish up Mounds of Memories and Culinary Delights,'" *Charlotte Observer*, Section: Gaston, Commentary, section I, page 1.

5. Rebecca Clark, "Cleveland County Residents Are Main Characters in Book about Broad River," *Shelby Star*, November 5, 2010.

6. Earl Scruggs, author interview, 1998.

7. Trish Camp, author telephone interview, December 2, 2014.

8. Béla Fleck and Tony Trischka, "Earl Scruggs [2006] interview," *Banjo Newsletter*, accessed May 2012.

9. Jesse McReynolds, author telephone interview, March 7, 2016.

10. Jim Mills, author interview, 2013.

11. Uncredited writer, "Earl Scruggs: Bluegrass Banjo Player," NEA National Heritage Fellowships, www.arts.gov/honors/heritage/fellows/earl-scruggs, accessed September 5, 2016.

Chapter 5. Joining Bill Monroe

1. Bill Monroe, author interview, Monroe office, Goodlettsville, Tennessee, 1986.

2. Earl Scruggs, telecast of reunion of Country Music Hall of Fame members, part of *Grand Ole Opry 65th Anniversary Show*, January 19, 1991.

3. Geoffrey Himes, "Earl Scruggs Stays Fresh through Long Career," *Chicago Tribune*, September 16, 2001.

4. Mac Wiseman, author interview, Antioch, Tennessee, 2004.

5. Béla Fleck, author telephone interview, December 15, 2015.

6. Earl Scruggs, author interview, 1989.

7. Charles Wolfe, interview with Monroe, *The Bluegrass Reader*, Thomas Goldsmith, editor, University of Illinois Press, Urbana, 2004.

8. Pete Wernick, "Bill Monroe and the Banjo," September 2011 column, *Banjo Newsletter*, September 2011. Wernick indicates in this column that Tony Trischka was interviewing Monroe during this section.

9. Bill Malone and Jocelyn R. Neal, *Country Music, USA*, University of Texas Press, Austin, revised edition, 2000, 327.

10. Steve Martin, author telephone interview, August 16, 2015.

11. Earl Scruggs and Bill Monroe, audiotape, Bill Monroe and the Bluegrass Boys at Bean Blossom, September 15, 1979. Quotes from Scruggs and Monroe on the early days are both from this show, where Scruggs made a guest appearance with the Blue Grass Boys.

Chapter 6. Working as a Blue Grass Boy

1. Jerry Douglas, author interview, March 18, 2016.

2. Earl Scruggs, author interview, 2007.

3. Pete Kuykendall, author interview, Raleigh, North Carolina, 2014.

4. Neil V. Rosenberg and Charles K. Wolfe, *The Music of Bill Monroe*, University of Illinois Press, Urbana, 2007, 61.

5. Jerry Keys, author interview, Knoxville, Tennessee, 2016.

6. Earl Scruggs, author interview, 2007.

7. Scruggs's comments on Monroe's lateness, etc., author interview, 2007.

8. Mac Wiseman, author telephone interview, 2015.

9. Earl Scruggs, author interview, 2007.

10. Paul Kingsbury, "Grand Ole Opry," *Encyclopedia of Country Music*, second edition, editors Paul Kingsbury, John W. Rumble, Michael McCall, Oxford University Press, New York, 2012, 194–195.

11. Larry Perkins, "The Book of Earl" Facebook site, May 5, 2014. Perkins, a notable banjo player, former Blue Grass Boy, and longtime Scruggs friend, reported that Scruggs gave a broad grin on hearing a tape of a transcription, made by an unidentified person, of himself playing "Cripple Creek" with Acuff. "Our Friends Jerry Steinberg and Gary Gregory shared this historic clip today," Perkins wrote on his site.

12. Curly Seckler, author interview, March 16, 2013.

Chapter 7. Flatt and Scruggs Build a Career

1. Earl Scruggs, *Earl Scruggs and the 5-String Banjo: Revised and Enhanced Edition*, Hal Leonard, Milwaukee, 2005, 165.

2. Béla Fleck, author telephone interview, December 10, 2015.

3. Curly Seckler, author interview, 2013.

4. Olive Dame Campbell and Cecil J. Sharp, *English Folk Songs from the Southern Appalachians: Comprising 122 Songs and Ballads, and 323 Tunes*, G. P. Putnam's Sons, New York, 1917, 204.

5. Barry Willis, "Earl Scruggs Biography," website, The Flatt and Scruggs Preservation Society—Established 1998, www.flatt-and-scruggs.com/earl-scruggs .html, accessed May 3, 2019.

6. Jesse McReynolds, author telephone interview, March 7, 2016.

7. Uncredited writer, "City Sells Nine Trailers for Average Price Of $130," *Kingsport News*, Kingsport, Tennessee, March 17, 1949, 7.

8. Jerry Keys, author interview, Knoxville, Tennessee, 2016.

9. Curly Seckler, author interview, 2013.

10. Mac Wiseman, author interview, 2015.

11. Curly Seckler, author interview, 2013.

12. Earl Scruggs and Louise Scruggs, informal author interviews.

13. Jim Mills, author interview, March 8, 2013.

14. Penny Parsons, email correspondence, 2015.

Chapter 8. Recording "Foggy Mountain Breakdown"

1. Thomas Goldsmith, "It Was the Singing: A Conversation with Mac Wiseman," *Bluegrass Unlimited*, February 2006, 24–27.

2. Marc Myers, "The Silence That Sparked New Sounds," *Wall Street Journal*, December 26, 2012.

3. John Rumble, "Murray Nash," *Encyclopedia of Country Music*, second edition, Paul Kingsbury, John W. Rumble, Michael McCall, editors, Oxford University Press, New York, 2012, 194–195.

4. Murray Nash, interview by John W. Rumble, Country Music Foundation Oral History Project, Country Music Hall of Fame and Museum, Nashville, Tennessee, June 13, 1983.

5. Uncredited writer, "Police Seek Link between Two Gang Slaying," *Chicago Tribune*, Chicago, Illinois, May 25, 1948, 8.

6. Nash, CMF interview, 1983.

7. jazzdisco.org, Mercury Records listing.

8. Over-the-Rhine Foundation website, "Early History," http://www.otrfoundation .org/OTR_History.htm, accessed Sept. 6, 2016.

9. "New Business Starts," *Cincinnati Enquirer*, March 26, 1946, 30.

10. Charlene Blevins, "Castle Studios—Nashville, Tennessee (1948)," June 1, 2004, www.pastemagazine.com/articles/2004/06/castle-studios-nashville-tennessee-1948.html, accessed May 3, 2019.

11. Uncredited author, "Music Row in Nashville," Audio Engineering Society.

12. Nash, CMF interview, 1983.

13. Steven Schoenherr, "The History of Magnetic Recording" (Background on Ampex, Magnecord) Audio Engineering Society website, University of San Diego, November 5, 2002.

14. Jon Hartley Fox, *King of the Queen City: The Story of King Records*, University of Illinois Press, Urbana, 2009, 54.

15. Penny Parsons, email correspondence, 2015.

16. Uncredited writer, "Clay-Gentry Gets Exclusive Rights for Barn Dance," *Lexington Leader*, Lexington, Kentucky, April 12, 1950.

17. Murray Nash, interview by Doug Green, May 15, 1974, Country Music Foundation Oral History Project, Country Music Hall of Fame and Museum, Nashville, Tennessee.

18. "Record Reviews," *Billboard*, New York, April 15, 1950, 120.

Chapter 9. "Like a Jackhammer"—How the Tune Works

1. Tim O'Brien, author telephone interview, 2014.

2. Earl Scruggs, author interview. All Scruggs quotes in this chapter are from the June 2007 interview focused on "Foggy Mountain Breakdown."

3. Chris Stewart, "Lester Flatt Style Rhythm Guitar Instruction Taught by Chris Sharp," uploaded November 27, 2008.

4. Jerry Douglas, author interview, 2016.

5. Greg Earnest, email to author, June 4, 2017.

6. Les McIntyre, "Portrait of a Forgotten Bluegrass Fiddler," *Bluegrass Unlimited*, October 1983.

7. Louie W. Atteberry, "Hoedown," *American Folklore: An Encyclopedia*, Jan Harold Brunvand, editor. Garland Publishing, Inc., New York, 1996, 774–776.

8. Samuel Clemens, *The Adventures of Huckleberry Finn*, www.gutenberg.org/files/76/76-h/76-h.htm, accessed May 8, 2019.

9. Charles Wolfe, "Bluegrass Touches—An Interview with Bill Monroe," *The Bluegrass Reader*, Thomas Goldsmith, editor, University of Illinois Press, Urbana, 2004, 80.

10. Jim Mills, author interview, March 8, 2013.

Chapter 10. The Number-One Banjo Player

1. Curly Seckler, author interview, 2013.

2. Grady Morton, "Hurricanes of the 1950 Season," *Monthly Weather Review*, Miami, Florida, 13–15.

3. Uncredited writer, "WDAE AM & FM—A History," www.radioyears.com/other/

details.cfm?id=431; www.radioyears.com/other/photo_details.cfm?photo=1583 &id=13, accessed May 2019.

4. Neil Rosenberg, email, April 25, 2019.

5. "Martha White Foods," *The Tennessee Encyclopedia of History and Culture, Online Edition, 2002–2015,* University of Tennessee Press, Knoxville.

6. Earl Scruggs, author interview, 2007.

7. Johnny Sippel, "Folk Talent and Tunes," *Billboard,* New York City, May 28, 1949, 32.

8. Uncredited writer, "Troy Martin: Biography," Allmusic.com, www.allmusic.com/artist/troy-martin-mn0000747484/biography, accessed May 2019.

9. Neil V. Rosenberg, liner notes to Bear Family CD set, 1990.

10. John Chapman, "State Season Gets Its Start on a 'Hayride,'" *Chicago Tribune,* Chicago, Illinois, September 13, 1954, Part 7, Section 2, 25.

11. David W. Johnson, *Lonesome Melodies: The Lives and Music of the Stanley Brothers,* University of Mississippi Press, Oxford, 2013, 134.

12. Bill Emerson, "Thanks, Chief: A Sonny Osborne Appreciation," banjonews.com/2007-09/thanks_chief_a_sonny_osborne_appreciation.html, accessed May 2019.

13. Bill C. Malone, *Music from the True Vine: Mike Seeger's Life and Musical Journey,* University of North Carolina Press, Chapel Hill, 2011, 46.

Chapter 11. *The Beverly Hillbillies* Welcomes the Banjo

1. Paul Cullum, "Paul Henning," *Encyclopedia of Television,* Horace Newcomb, editor, Museum of Broadcast Communications website.

2. Tom McCourt and Nabeel Zuberi, *Encyclopedia of Television,* Horace Newcomb, editor, Museum of Broadcast Communications website.

3. Advertisement, *Billboard,* May 13, 1950, 33.

4. Archie Green, letter to Mrs. Earl Scruggs, Archie Green collection, UNC–Chapel Hill Southern Folklife Collection, folder "Scruggs, Earl and Louise," February 12, 1963.

5. Bill Yaryan, "Jazz, and All That: Folk Music Fans Have Full Summer," *Pasadena Star-News,* Pasadena, California, June 10, 1962, 74.

6. "Screenwriting from Iowa . . . and Other Unlikely Places" blog, "The Beverly Hills—Ozarks Connection," wordpress.com, January 29, 2014.

7. Richard Carlin, *Country Music: A Biographical Dictionary,* Routledge, New York, 2014, 27.

8. Karen Linn, *That Half-Barbaric Twang: The Banjo in American Popular Culture,* University of Illinois, Urbana, 1994, 142.

9. Ibid., 87.

10. Alice Gerrard, author interview, October 1, 2015.

11. Neil V. Rosenberg, *Bluegrass: A History,* University of Illinois Press, Urbana, 1985, 182.

12. Josh Graves and Fred Bartenstein, *Bluegrass Bluesman,* University of Illinois, Urbana, 2012, 43.

Chapter 12. Riding with Bonnie and Clyde

1. Steve Martin, author telephone interview, August 16, 2015.

2. Wes Heibling, "End of the Road for Bonnie & Clyde," *Bastrop Daily Enterprise*, Bastrop, Texas, January 3, 2012.

3. "Bonnie and Clyde—FBI," website; www.fbi.gov/about-us/history/famous-cases/bonnie-and-clyde, accessed September 10, 2016.

4. John Toland, *The Dillinger Days*, Da Capo Press, Lebanon, Indiana, 1963, 315.

5. "A Guide to the Robert Benton Papers 1969—1994," Robert Benton Papers, Southwestern Writers Collection 096, Texas State University–San Marcos, San Marcos, Texas.

6. Patrick Goldstein, "Blasts from the Past, *Bonnie and Clyde* Caught Many Off Guard (Jack Warner, for One) in '67. Here, the Stars and Others Look Back," Calendar, *Los Angeles Times*, Los Angeles, California, August 24, 1997.

7. Uncredited writer, "Country Music Show," *Gaffney Ledger*, Gaffney, South Carolina, March, 1967, 1.

8. Bosley Crowther, "*Bonnie and Clyde*," *New York Times*, August 14, 1967.

9. Peter Biskind, *Star: How Warren Beatty Seduced America*, Simon and Schuster, New York City, 2010, 128.

10. Pauline Kael, "Onward and Upward with the Arts," *Bonnie and Clyde*, *The New Yorker*, October 21, 1967, 147.

11. Roger Ebert, "*Bonnie and Clyde* Starts War of the Critics," *San Antonio Express–News*, San Antonio, Texas, November 26, 1967, 6-H.

12. *Time* cover, *Time* staff, "Hollywood: The Shock of Freedom in Films," December 8, 1967.

13. Jack Hurst and Kathy Gallagher, "Two Grammys for Russell, Cash, Redding," *The Tennessean*, Nashville, March 13, 1969, 6.

14. Robert Benton, author interview, 2015.

Chapter 13. Scruggs without Flatt

1. NBC press release re Flatt and Scruggs on float, January 1969.

2. Robert Johnson, "Steve Martin: A Man and His Banjo," *My San Antonio*, San Antonio, Texas, August 26, 2011.

3. Uncredited writer, "Flatt and Scruggs Are Appearing in Meadville," *The News-Herald*, Franklin, Pennsylvania, February 8, 1969, 2.

4. United Press International, "Flatt, Scruggs Split," *Statesville Record and Landmark*, Statesville, North Carolina, April 14, 1969, 16.

5. Jack Hurst, "Lawsuits Dropped by Flatt and Scruggs," *The Tennessean*, Nashville, December 2, 1969, 1.

6. Ron Clingen, "Ron Clingen's The Country Beat," *The Journal*, Ottawa, Ontario, Canada, 26.

7. Josh Graves and Fred Bartenstein, editor, *Bluegrass Bluesman: A Memoir*, University of Illinois Press, Urbana, 2012.

8. United Press International, "Bluegrass Loses Star," *Democrat-Times*, Greenville, Mississippi, July 24, 1972, 9.

9. Uncredited writer, "Ask Them Yourself," *The Progress*, Clearfield, Pennsylvania, November 27, 1971, 14.

10. Alan Wilson, Associated Press, "Banjoist Earl Scruggs Wins Acclaim with New Sound," *Chillicothe Constitution-Tribune*, Chillicothe, Ohio, December 26, 1972, 27.

11. Geoffrey Himes, "Earl Scruggs Stays Fresh through Long Career," *Chicago Tribune*, Chicago, Illinois, September 16, 2001.

12. Perry Meisel, email, January 21, 2016.

13. Wilhelm Murg, "Rhiannon Giddens: Pure Folk-Music Fire from 'A Good-Ol' Mixed Race North Carolinian,'" Indian Country Media Network, https://news maven.io/indiancountrytoday/archive/rhiannon-giddens-pure-folk-fire-from-a -good-ol-mixed-race-north-carolinian-NqIofOsY30OCsZ1t5rspxw/, accessed May 11, 2019.

14. Ron Clingen, "Country Music Spectacular Sets Ottawa a-Swingin'," *The Ottawa Journal*, May 23, 1969, 44.

15. David Hoffman, director, *Earl Scruggs: The Bluegrass Legend—Family & Friends*, 1972.

16. Olof Bjorner, website, www.bjorner.com, accessed July 17, 2016.

17. Paula Underwood, email to author, November 5, 2015.

18. Tom Roland, website, "Roland Note, The Ultimate Country Music Database," https://www.rolandnote.com, accessed July 17, 2016.

19. Alan Munde, author telephone interview, November 7, 2015.

20. Thomas Goldsmith, liner notes for boxed set, *Flatt on Victor Plus More*, Bear Family Records, December 7, 1999.

Chapter 14. Scruggs's Banjo Gains a Cult Following

1. *Gibson Guitars-Banjos-Mandolins-Ukuleles*, 1930–1931 catalog, Gibson Inc., Kalamazoo, Michigan, 22–23.

2. Alan Munde, author interview, November 7, 2015.

3. Greg Earnest, "Gibson RB-Granada Mastertone #9584-3, the 'Earl Scruggs,'" www.earnestbanjo.com/gibson_banjo_RB-granada_mastertone_9584-3.htm, accessed July 17, 2016.

4. Greg Deering, "Banjo Buying Tips," https://www.deeringbanjos.com/blogs/ banjo-buying-tips/10319001-deering-banjo-tone-ring-comparisons, accessed June 3, 2017.

5. Joe Spann, "The Banjos of Earl Scruggs—Part2," Banjo Café, http://www.banjocafe .net/forum/content.php?148-The-Banjos-of-Earl-Scruggs-Part-1, accessed May 11, 2019.

Chapter 15. Reaping the Harvest

1. Barry R. Willis, "Scruggs Bio," http://www.flatt-and-scruggs.com/earlbio. html, accessed December 9, 2015.

2. Jerry Douglas, author interview, Nashville, Tennessee, March 2016.

3. John Gardner, email interview, November 2, 2015.

4. Phil Hood, editor, "Bill Monroe," *Artists of American Folk Music*, William Morrow, New York, 1987, 28.

5. Tommy Goldsmith, "Bill Monroe and Earl Scruggs: Together Again," *Bluegrass Unlimited*, September 1994, 8–9.

6. Muriel Anderson, Facebook post, March 30, 2012.

7. Peter Wernick, "Notes from the Road," www.drbanjo.com/notesfromtheroad/notesfrmrd27.html, accessed February 6, 2015.

8. A shortened version of the music from the Beatty tribute is at https://www.youtube.com/watch?v=vggHy_Qt5-c, accessed May 13, 2019.

9. Steve Martin, author telephone interview, August 16, 2015. All subsequent Martin quotes are from this interview.

10. Steve Martin, "The Master from Flint Hill: Earl Scruggs," *The New Yorker*, January 13, 2012.

11. Bill Evans, blog post, billevansbanjo.com/blog/remembering-earl-scruggs, posted July 3, 2012, accessed December 13, 2015.

12. Jerry Douglas, author telephone interview, December 11, 2015.

INDEX

THOMAS GOLDSMITH is a journalist and musician. For more than thirty years, he has worked both in daily newspapers in North Carolina and Tennessee and as a freelance writer. He is the editor of *The Bluegrass Reader*, winner of the International Bluegrass Music Association's best journalist award.

MUSIC IN AMERICAN LIFE

Songprints: The Musical Experience of Five Shoshone Women   *Judith Vander*

"Happy in the Service of the Lord": Afro-American Gospel Quartets in
   Memphis   *Kip Lornell*

Paul Hindemith in the United States   *Luther Noss*

"My Song Is My Weapon": People's Songs, American Communism, and the Politics
   of Culture, 1930–50   *Robbie Lieberman*

Chosen Voices: The Story of the American Cantorate   *Mark Slobin*

Theodore Thomas: America's Conductor and Builder of Orchestras, 1835–
   1905   *Ezra Schabas*

"The Whorehouse Bells Were Ringing" and Other Songs Cowboys Sing
   Collected and Edited by Guy Logsdon

Crazeology: The Autobiography of a Chicago Jazzman   *Bud Freeman,
   as Told to Robert Wolf*

Discoursing Sweet Music: Brass Bands and Community Life in Turn-of-the-Century
   Pennsylvania   *Kenneth Kreitner*

Mormonism and Music: A History   *Michael Hicks*

Voices of the Jazz Age: Profiles of Eight Vintage Jazzmen   *Chip Deffaa*

Pickin' on Peachtree: A History of Country Music in Atlanta, Georgia
   Wayne W. Daniel

Bitter Music: Collected Journals, Essays, Introductions, and Librettos
   Harry Partch; edited by Thomas McGeary

Ethnic Music on Records: A Discography of Ethnic Recordings Produced in the
   United States, 1893 to 1942   *Richard K. Spottswood*

Downhome Blues Lyrics: An Anthology from the Post–World War II Era
   Jeff Todd Titon

Ellington: The Early Years   *Mark Tucker*

Chicago Soul   *Robert Pruter*

That Half-Barbaric Twang: The Banjo in American Popular Culture   *Karen Linn*

Hot Man: The Life of Art Hodes   *Art Hodes and Chadwick Hansen*

The Erotic Muse: American Bawdy Songs (2d ed.)   *Ed Cray*

Barrio Rhythm: Mexican American Music in Los Angeles   *Steven Loza*

The Creation of Jazz: Music, Race, and Culture in Urban America   *Burton W. Peretti*

Charles Martin Loeffler: A Life Apart in Music   *Ellen Knight*

Club Date Musicians: Playing the New York Party Circuit   *Bruce A. MacLeod*

Opera on the Road: Traveling Opera Troupes in the United States,
   1825–60   *Katherine K. Preston*

The Stonemans: An Appalachian Family and the Music That Shaped Their
   Lives   *Ivan M. Tribe*

Transforming Tradition: Folk Music Revivals Examined   *Edited by Neil V. Rosenberg*

The Crooked Stovepipe: Athapaskan Fiddle Music and Square Dancing in Northeast
   Alaska and Northwest Canada   *Craig Mishler*

Traveling the High Way Home: Ralph Stanley and the World of Traditional
   Bluegrass Music   *John Wright*

Carl Ruggles: Composer, Painter, and Storyteller   *Marilyn Ziffrin*

Never without a Song: The Years and Songs of Jennie Devlin, 1865–1952
   Katharine D. Newman

The University of Illinois Press
is a founding member of the
Association of University Presses.

Composed in 10.25/14 Chaparral Pro
with Dabre Grunge and Amber Whiskey display
by Lisa Connery
at the University of Illinois Press
Cover designed by Dustin J. Hubbart
Cover illustration: Scruggs played a Gibson RB-11 banjo
during his years with Bill Monroe.
Photo courtesy Jim Mills Collection.
Manufactured by Sheridan Books, Inc.

University of Illinois Press
1325 South Oak Street
Champaign, IL 61820-6903
www.press.uillinois.edu